The Oskar Davidsen book of
OPEN SANDWICHES

compiled by James R. White
from traditional Danish recipes
and specialities of the House
of Oskar Davidsen

HØST & SØNS FORLAG

COPENHAGEN

© *Høst & Søns Forlag 1955. Printed in Denmark*
by S. L. Møllers Bogtrykkeri, Copenhagen. 4th edition 1965.

For those who might ask to what extent this book has been sponsored or subsidized by any person or firm the answer, rather sadly, is: not at all. No such sponsorship, advertising or other form of subsidy was even sought.

COVER: *On the plate: Roast beef and remoulade (No. 62). On the dish: Parboiled egg with caviar (No. 138), Hans Andersen's Favourite (No. 48), Shrimps, pyramid portion (No. 5), Danablu cheese with a raw egg yolk (No. 171).*

FRONTISPIECE: *On the plate: Salmon with asparagus and spinach (page 73). On the dish: Smoked eel with scrambled egg (No. 19), Lobster with curry-mayonnaise (No. 14), Union Jack Sandwich (No. 54), Luncheon sausage with meat jelly (No. 126), Tomato and egg.*

Looking back . . .

Once upon a time in Old Copenhagen there lived a wine merchant named Oskar Davidsen. To his cellars, to sample the many good things which he stocked, men came from far and wide. As they tasted they often became hungry. Which is why Oskar's wife, Petrea, won a niche in the Hall of Fame. In a back room she used to prepare dainty snacks for the customers. This was some 75 years ago. The business prospered and 15 years later Oskar's son Vagn Aage Davidsen took it over. Subsequently, under the management of the late Axel Svensson and of Per Davidsen, grandson of Oskar, the fame of the House of Davidsen spread beyond Scandinavia, beyond Europe even.

That was the position when this book was published. Soon the book found its way to the United States where Miss Ida Davidsen, the daughter of Per, was already making a name for herself and Danish sandwiches at Hollywood's "Scandia" restaurant on Sunset Boulevard. Further south the wife of the commanding general at Cape Canaveral was photographed clutching the book as she explained that whenever she wanted to give her husband and other top brass a special treat she made Danish sandwiches for them.

Back in Europe the British European Airways manager in Lisbon was presenting the B.E.A. catering manager with a copy of the book and emphasising the advantages of Danish sandwiches for passenger snacks. Soon B.E.A. became *smørrebrød*-minded and Miss Ida Davidsen was given a year's contract to initiate B.E.A. caterers throughout Europe and the Middle East into the mysteries of Danish open sandwiches.

Today Miss Ida is back at the House of Davidsen, carrying on the work begun by great grandmother Petrea Davidsen.

Lisbon, 1962　　　　　　　　　　　　　　JAMES R. WHITE

FOREWORD TO THE 4TH EDITION

Since 1962, when the 3rd edition of this book was published, the fame of Danish *smørrebrød* (open-faced sandwiches) has spread more and more – thanks in no small measure to the thousands of tourists who have acquired a taste for this Danish speciality. Many have been the calls from abroad for the services of Danish specialists in this sphere of culinary art, and Per Davidsen and his daughter Ida have travelled widely as ambassadors of Danish *smørrebrød.*

In 1962 a Danish Food Festival was arranged in Chicago, and shortly afterwards there was a similar arrangement in conjunction with a big American department store.

Ida Davidsen has demonstrated Danish *smørrebrød* and given instruction in their preparation in a chain of British coffee-shops and restaurants and in the course of a tour through Canada.

Brazil has also shown keen interest in Danish *smørrebrød*, with the result that Ida Davidsen, with assistance of a small staff from the Oskar Davidsen restaurant in Copenhagen, has helped to start up a Scandinavian restaurant in Sao Paulo. And as these lines are being written, an Oskar Davidsen restaurant is being prepared in Minneapolis as part of a Scandinavian Center being planned in that city.

HØST & SØNS FORLAG

Contents

What is Smørrebrød?

Smørrebrød can be anything between heaven and earth. Primarily it consists of a piece of bread of some kind. The Danes make most use of rye bread because it is more suitable than other varieties for many of their sandwiches. It also contains more vitamin B than wheaten bread. But many other kinds of bread, most of them more readily available outside Scandinavia than rye bread, can be used (see page 13).

Upon the bread something, generally butter, is in most cases spread. As one would expect, when the Danes spread the fine butter for which they are famous, they spread it generously. Not only because it gives them vitamin A or because they like the taste but also because fatstuffs help to keep out the cold. And keeping out the cold is important for most of the Danish year.

Though butter ranks first as "the something to spread", spiced lard or pork dripping, maybe even goose or duck dripping, are often used. Not only, in the case of the pork fat, as an economy measure but because the Danes prefer fat to butter when liverpaste, salt meats and most kinds of sausage, are to be the crowning glory of the *smørrebrød*.

When it comes to the question of what to put on the "buttered bread" (the Danish words for "butter" and "to butter" are the same as for "grease" and "to grease" so the expression "buttered bread" includes bread spread with dripping of one kind or another) the only answer can be: "There is absolutely nothing edible which cannot be used for *smørrebrød*".

The Danish town housewife patronises the charcuterie or cooked meat shop around the corner; her country sister may buy certain kinds of *pålæg* (literally "something laid on", i. e. any fish, meat, vegetable etc. used on the buttered bread) from the butcher who brings his mobile shop to her door, but she will make most of her requirements in her own kitchen, most frequently using home-killed pigs for the raw materials. Above all both town and country housewife will make use of leftovers for *pålæg*. "Leftovers" embraces anything from slices of cold pork sausage garnished with a remnant of red cabbage to slices taken from a still substantial joint of meat.

It is this use of leftovers which makes *smørrebrød* such a useful thing to know about in order to be able to cope in an interesting yet substantial manner with those unexpected guests. On page 57 will be found some suggestions as to how one can serve an excellent evening snack with the aid of leftovers in the refrigerator or larder, or even a more ambitious supper if there are a few cans of fish or meat in the store cupboard and a few jars of pickles, or fresh tomatoes or cucumber to hand.

The average Dane has only one hot meal daily. For lunch and/or supper he eats *smørrebrød*. In Copenhagen and other towns most people take their hot meal in the evening, in the country it is usual to eat it at midday. To take lunch at a restaurant is unusual in Denmark, unless business is involved. Nearly all, from the labourer who eats his at the side of the road to the managing director who has his at his desk, take a home-made *smørrebrød* pack with them when they go to work in the morning. Others buy their sandwiches at special shops on their way to office or factory. However they come by it, a sandwich lunch makes it possible for both worker and executive to limit their lunch "hour" to thirty minutes and thus give themselves more time for work—or play.

The Sandwich Story

Somewhere in the centre of Copenhagen there ought to be a monument to the man or woman who discovered *smørrebrød*, the open sandwich which is Denmark's national dish. An appropriate site would be the Town Hall end of the new Hans Andersen Boulevard, for the inventor of *smørrebrød* obviously had something of the fantasy of the great Danish storyteller. Alas, historians are silent as to the identity of the man who first placed fish, fowl, meat and vegetables on a piece of buttered bread. Some Danish encyclopedias do not even list one of the most important words in the Danish language.

The inventor of the *smørrebrødsseddel* or sandwich list is, however (see page 12), known. And nobody has ever disputed that it was not until old Oskar Davidsen acceded to the request of young Axel Svensson to be allowed to make somthing amusing out of the restaurant's sandwich list that open sandwiches in all their infinite variety began to develop into what they are today.

Maybe no monument to Axel Svensson will be raised during this century for, when it comes to paying tribute to their own sons, the Danes are not an impetuous people. It took them several generations to accept the genius of Hans Andersen and it was not until the storyteller's potentialities as a tourist attraction were conceived that his greatness was fully acknowledged. But in the case of Axel Svensson the position is different for the fame of the *smørrebrød* composed by him, those glorious symphonies of colour and delectability, has long since become a major tourist attraction.

The origin of the sandwich is a subject on which even the historians can but speculate. Some suggest that recognisable sandwiches were known in ancient Babylon, others that a rabbi contrived them for the Passover by placing bitter herbs between two slices of unleavened bread to symbolise Jewish privations in Egypt.

When *smørrebrød* first saw the light of day is equally a matter for speculation. Certainly it appeared centuries before an Earl of Sandwich first placed pieces of meat between *two* slices of bread to enable his guests to eat without leaving the card table.

The Danish word means simply "buttered bread". But the origins of open sandwiches can be traced back to the days when, in Denmark as elsewhere, a round of bread served as a plate for both hot food and cold. Naturally the rich refrained from eating their plates but these, soaked in nourishing gravy from the main course, invariably found their way to the mouths of the serfs or deserving poor of the parish. And between rich and poor there was doubtless a class which ate both bread-plate and the delicacies which reposed upon it.

As yet, however, this open sandwich could not have been known as *smørrebrød* for butter was still unknown in Denmark. Incidentally butter is first mentioned by Moses (Deut. ch. *32*, verse *14*).

The earliest mention of the word *smørrebrød* is found in the works of the playwright Ludvig Holberg (1684–1754) who describes the diet of the gentry as consisting of soup, salt meat or *smørrebrød*.

No mystery, however, surrounds the invention of the *smørrebrødsseddel* or printed list of open sandwiches. It was Emil Bjørn, head waiter at the Copenhagen officers' club, who, when harried by shouted orders from the card tables, conceived, in 1883, the idea of lists on which the guests could mark off their requirements.

Bjørn's idea was soon adopted by restaurants throughout the country, but many years were to pass before these scant lists were developed into what they are in Denmark today.

Bread

The Danes have a wide choice of bread, ranging from rye bread (light, dark, wholemeal and others) via sour bread and *sigtebrød* to various kinds of wheaten bread and crispbread made of rye.

Nearly all *smørrebrød* is, in fact, eaten on one of the three rye bread types. This is the Dane's staff of life and the thing which he misses above all others if he goes abroad or lives in one of the many countries which do not bake such bread. Most people not born in Scandinavia but in countries where rye bread is not eaten are inclined to call it "black bread" and to dismiss it as something eaten only by those who cannot afford or obtain other kinds of bread. They are quite wrong and should at least give rye bread a trial.

Some Danes eat even shrimps and cheese on rye bread but these are more often eaten on wheaten bread, preferably a variety with a good crust.

Rye bread is for practical reasons that best suited for many kinds of open sandwich. Being harder and closer of texture than most sorts of wheaten bread, it does not, except when too fresh (should be a day or two old) crumble when spread. This hardness of texture often plays an important part in the balance of the *smørrebrød*, as a good general rule is that soft varieties of *pålæg* are best eaten on a hard bread and vice-versa.

If you do acquire a loaf of genuine Danish ryebread, it should be cut in slices not more than an eighth of an inch thick. Every Danish home has a special machine to cut rye bread, as to do so with a knife is by no means easy if the slice is to be even— which it must be for the sake of appearance at least.

More frequently found outside Denmark than Danish rye bread is the German variety. "Jaus *Rheinisches Vollkornbrot*", sliced and available in packets or tins, is excellent. The Danes seldom use sweet "*pumpernickel*" rye bread and then only with cheese.

As a general alternative to rye bread, toasted wheaten bread is recommended. Toasting holds the bread together and makes it more suitable, for example, for use with soft varieties of *pålæg* such as liverpaste. Moreover butter is not absorbed by cold toast (never butter this for *smørrebrød* until it is cold) as it is by fresh wheaten bread. It is most important that the bread should be slightly toasted only. It must not be allowed to become hard.

An alternative to toast as a substitute for rye bread is crispbread. An advantage of this is that it can be stored for weeks. Accordingly it often makes its appearance in Danish homes simultaneously with the arrival of unexpected guests. When served the pieces should not be larger than the area of two matchboxes. This will probably mean halving the piece that comes out of the packet. Often found, and excellent, on crispbread are *gaffelbidder* (Danish spiced herring tit-bits), liverpaste, salami and cheese. Also useful for daily, or emergency, sandwiches are crackers or biscuits of the wholemeal, digestive, marie or petit beurre types.

The most usual form of Danish wheaten bread is known as a "French loaf". Although the top is rounded, the bottom of the loaf is flat and the whole thing is about a foot long. It is crusty though not quite as crusty as those French loaves which you buy by the yard in France.

When standard local loaves of wheaten bread are used, those yielding a square slice will be found most useful for open sandwiches. And a *small* loaf will give a less clumsy slice than a large loaf.

The Oskar Davidsen Sandwich List

Writers from Britain and the United States have often claimed that the Davidsen sandwich list is the world's longest. No such claim has ever been advanced by anyone connected with the Oskar Davidsen concern. But though the claim has frequently appeared in such widely circulated publications as "Esquire" and "The Saturday Evening Post", to say nothing of practically every one of the larger newspapers in the United States and United Kingdom, it has never been challenged.

But the fame of the 4-foot long sandwich list, of which 500,000 copies have been given away since the war, does not rest so much on its length as on its contents. These are examined at length in the following pages.

Fish, Shellfish, [etc.]

1 DANISH CAVIAR ON TOAST

Danish caviar is not sturgeon roe but that of the lumpfish which the dictionary describes as "an uncouth spiny-finned leaden-blue fish clinging tightly to objects by a sucking-disk on its belly". Ugly though the fish may be, both its flesh and roe are excellent—and cheap. The sandwich is decorated with a piece of lemon cut to the centre and twisted so that it can stand upright and, maybe, with chopped hardboiled egg.

2 SHRIMPS

It needs a poet—or a Dane—to describe the Danish shrimp. As a description has been attempted on page 76 it is unnecessary to say more here except to remark that at Davidsen's no lettuce leaf is inserted between the thickly-buttered wheaten bread and the shrimps. No. 2 is just a small portion of shrimps. Even so these have to be stood on their shoulders and tails to be accommodated on a single slice of bread.

3 SHRIMPS, DOUBLE PORTION

This is as above but the number of shrimps has now risen to 45—55.

4 THE RUSH HOUR

This consists of a double layer of shrimps with two extra rows of shrimps atop. On this sandwich there are 80—100 shrimps.

5 SHRIMPS, PYRAMID PORTION

Here the Davidsen shrimp orgy reaches its climax. The shrimps, with their tails and shoulders resting upon the butter, tightly packed together in rows, completely cover the bread as usual. Above the first layer of shrimps comes a second, with a row less on the outside and without going quite to the ends of the bread. The superimposed rows continue until the pyramid is complete.

6 PARBOILED EGG IN MAYONNAISE WITH SHRIMPS

The egg is boiled for 6—7 minutes according to size and then halved and laid on rye bread. The egg is masked with mayonnaise and garnished with a zig-zag of shrimps.

7 SMOKED SALMON

Served on wheaten or rye bread, Davidsen's smoked salmon (discussed on page 73) is really something to remember. Cress, often used to embellish smoked salmon elsewhere, is banned here. Salt must never be used on smoked salmon, use coarse black pepper if you must season.

8 SMOKED SALMON WITH RAW EGG YOLK

The egg yolk, which reclines on the salmon, is broken and spread before eating. A ring of onion, often used to keep an egg yolk from running away, is not suitable here. A ring of tomato with the centre scooped out is used instead.

9 SMOKED SALMON WITH SCRAMBLED EGG

The egg, the making of which is described on page 92, is placed on the sandwich as a diagonal stripe.

10 SMOKED SALMON WITH STEWED MUSHROOMS

The mushrooms are cooked à la crème. This recipe is international and can be found in most good cookery books. See also page 99.

11 PURÉE OF SMOKED SALMON WITH RAW EGG YOLK, HORSERADISH AND ONION

Here for the second time we have that famous Davidsen raw egg yolk which we shall meet many times—both here and at other restaurants. The combination of smoked salmon, horseradish and raw onion is daring but successful.

12 LOBSTER, FRESHLY BOILED

From the end of May to mid-September the best lobsters in Denmark come from the North Sea coast of Jutland, being landed at Hirtshals. At other times they come from Norway or Sweden.

13 LOBSTER MAYONNAISE

This is the usual way to serve lobster as *smørrebrød*. It is worth remembering that the coral red roe of the female lobster is not only decorative but good eating. Chopped parsley usually lingers lovingly in the neighbourhood of any Danish lobster.

14 LOBSTER WITH CURRY-MAYONNAISE

Here the famous Svensson fantasy gets under way. You will probably agree with him that a little curry suits lobster extremely well. And a couple of slices of tomato look decorative without detracting from the delicate flavour. Curry-mayonnaise described on page 97.

15 LOBSTER WITH ASPARAGUS IN MAYONNAISE

Slices of tomato are equally in place here but curry would spoil the fine flavour of the asparagus.

16 LOBSTER WITH LETTUCE, SLICED EGG AND MAYONNAISE

The lettuce and sliced egg are here used with the mayonnaise out of respect for digestive organs which have difficulty in dealing with unrelieved lobster meat.

17 LOBSTER, CHOPPED HEART OF LETTUCE
AND RAW EGG YOLK ON TOAST

Here again consideration to the dyspeptic takes the form of lettuce. The combination of raw egg yolk and lettuce is an inspired one.

OPPOSITE: *On the plate: Fillet of plaice with luxury garnish (No. 24).*
On the dish: Collared pork (No. 116).
Salami with sliced potatoes and chives (No. 125).
Sardine with anchovies and fried egg (No. 82).
Clipper Sandwich (No. 47), Brisket of beef and horseradish (No. 73).

18 SIX SPLIT CRAWFISH TAILS WITH DILL-MAYONNAISE

These small freshwater "lobsters" are, perhaps because tradition calls for a *snaps* with each, Sweden's national dish. Dill is a herb of which too little is seen in many countries. The crawfish are cooked in water salted and flavoured with dill. The mayonnaise contains finely chopped dill.

In the former case the "crown" or flower of the dill plant is used, in the latter the chopped green leaves only. The crawfish are eaten cold. As usual beer accompanies the *snaps*. Or, if you really want to go to town, Bass ale mixed with dry champagne!

19 EEL, FRESHLY SMOKED, WITH SCRAMBLED EGG

Silver eel are best. They are, it seems, just right for eating when they are old enough for parenthood at the age of four, five or six. Until they reach this stage they are yellow-bellied. When they have reached it they are ready to head for their breeding grounds in the Sargasso Sea. Scandinavia eels are best in September, October and November. The experts declare that an eel ought to weigh a little over 1 lb. if the pieces are to be large enough to make a decent sandwich.

20 EEL WITH SCRAMBLED EGG, SPINACH AND FRIED MUSHROOMS

is described by its creator as "just a little joke" and needs no further explanation. It is an example of the way in which seemingly irreconcilable ingredients can be mated to form a harmonious whole.

2

21 FRIED FILLET OF PLAICE AND LEMON

Only cod is a close rival of plaice for the title of Denmark's national fish. The best plaice, according to tradition at least, are caught by the fishermen of Frederikshavn, on the Kattegat shore of North Jutland, between that port and the island of Læsø. At Davidsen's the fillets, after being dipped in beaten egg, are coated with a mixture of flour and browned bread-crumbs or cracker crumbs and then fried in deep fat. Sole is a rarity in Denmark but the more charitable Danes can be persuaded to admit that "sole is quite as good as plaice".

22 FRIED FILLET OF PLAICE AND REMOULADE

Danish remoulade (see page 100) differs from generally accepted varieties in that it does not contain hardboiled egg but does contain herbs like a sauce tartare. A quick remoulade is made by chopping some piccalilli finely and mixing with a not-too-thick mayonnaise.

23 DRESSED FRIED FILLET OF PLAICE

Here the fillets are not only served with remoulade but are decorated with pieces of asparagus laid across them. In be-tween these are placed shrimps and lobster or maybe strips of smoked salmon are laid criss-crossing the asparagus. According to season there will also be a small piece of tomato or lemon and maybe some mushrooms fried in butter.

24 FILLET OF PLAICE WITH DE LUXE GARNISH

This is a real find for the hostess in search of a novel and decorative lunch dish or fish course at dinner. Lettuce leaves are first placed upon the buttered bread. Upon the lettuce four fillets of plaice are placed on end to form a pyramid. A round of fried cod's roe (see page 90) is often placed inside the pyramid to support its base. The fillets are garnished with the ingredients mentioned under No. 23. Three Danes once betted with a fourth who claimed he could eat eight of these so-called high sandwiches. The boaster gave up after five.

25 PORTUGUESE SARDINE IN OIL

No Scandinavian holds the humble "brisling-sardine", caught in northern waters, in any high esteem. He insists on what he believes to be the only genuine sardine, that caught in southern waters and canned in France or Portugal.

The sardine should be old and well matured in olive oil. If you want to add colour to what might otherwise be a rather drab sandwich, decorate with tomato or lemon, cut to the centre and twisted maybe, and maybe a spiral of olive.

26 PORTUGUESE SARDINE AND 4 BONED ANCHOVIES IN OYSTER SAUCE

This much-imitated Davidsen speciality makes an excellent prelude to many a meal. Its popularity is due to the contrast between the fat, oily sardine and the salty, spicy anchovies. *Gaffelbidder*, the Danish spiced herring tit-bits, can be used instead of anchovies. This sandwich is best with toast.

27 PICKLED HERRING TIT-BITS WITH RAW ONION

The pickled herring is the delicious *gaffelbidder* mentioned above. The onion is chopped.

2*

28 POTATO SALAD WITH PICKLED HERRING TIT-BITS AND SEASONED BEETROOT

The potato salad is the normal variety consisting of potato in mayonnaise with a little finely chopped onion or chives. Finely chopped pickles can be used instead of beetroot.

29 PICKLED HERRING (OSKAR DAVIDSEN'S SPECIAL)

This is made with spiced Icelandic herring. Unlike ordinary pickled herrings these are not soaked in water before being prepared but in milk where they remain for 4—5 hours as otherwise they would taste too salt. They are scraped, the bones are removed and they are then put, in halves or smaller pieces, in white wine vinegar which has been well thinned down with water. The addition to the vinegar of a little oil makes the herring look pleasantly shiny. The herring is served with chopped onion.

30 FISHCAKE AND CAPERS

Perhaps the main attraction of the Danish fishcake is that it is comparatively inexpensive. It is made by scraping the fish from the skin and then pounding it with flour and milk before frying. On *smørrebrød* the fishcakes are sliced.

31 FISHCAKE AND REMOULADE

Add remoulade to even the humble fishcake and you've got, if not a dish fit for a king at least a reasonable sandwich.

32 FRESHLY SMOKED HERRING

Tradition, backed up by high-powered publicity, claims that the smoked herrings which come from the Baltic island of

Bornholm are best. Experts contend that equally fine herrings are smoked elsewhere in Denmark. Tradition rightly claims that the best wood over which the herring can be smoked is juniper.

Per Davidsen insists that no smoked herring in the world can compare with those of Bornholm. "Many foreign visitors, Americans in particular, come to Denmark in the season (summer months) for the sole reason of eating smoked Bornholm herrings at Oskar Davidsen's." That is Mr. Davidsen's story and he is sticking to it. Presumably the outstanding quality of the herring is due to the short distances the herring has to travel from the smokehouse.

33 FRESHLY SMOKED HERRING WITH RAW EGG YOLK

The egg yolk is prevented from wandering by being placed in an onion ring which has been laid upon the herring fillets. The yolk is broken and smeared over the fillets by the guest.

34 FRESHLY SMOKED HERRING WITH RAW EGG YOLK AND CHOPPED RADISHES

The accent is rightly on the "freshly smoked" as few things are more disappointing than a dry, several-day-old, smoked herring.

Delicacies like smoked herring must be served absolutely fresh. That's why it is best to eat them at the big restaurants which specialize in *smørrebrød* and get frequent supplies, sometimes several times daily.

Before leaving smoked herring the combination of these with scrambled egg or slices of parboiled egg with a wide border of finely chopped chives is worth noting.

35 THIN STRIPS OF ANCHOVY, BEETROOT, RAW EGG YOLK, CAPERS, ONION AND HORSERADISH

Like Scandinavian "sardines", the Scandinavian anchovy is, it seems, brisling. In this sandwich the anchovies are laid side by side with strips of beetroot and shavings of horseradish placed at right-angles to them. The raw egg is placed in an onion ring and the whole is garnished with chopped onion and capers.

This sandwich is in great demand as a lunchtime starter after a heavy night. The "cure" is completed by an icy *snaps* and an equally cold Carlsberg or Tuborg lager beer. Both this sandwich and numbers 36, 37, 38, 39 and 40 are particularly easy and quick to prepare even when the housewife isn't suffering from a husband with a hangover.

36 4 BONED ANCHOVIES IN OYSTER SAUCE

Even anchovies receive personal treatment at Davidsens. The fresh anchovies are placed in a top-secret oyster-anchovy pickle and kept there until required when the bones are removed and the fish cut into the finest strips.

This *smørrebrød*, say the Davidsens, is the simplest and easiest possible form of *hors d'oeuvres* if the main course is to be spaghetti, a rice or curry dish. The base for this sandwich should preferably be toast.

37 4 BONED ANCHOVIES WITH RAW EGG YOLK AND CHIVES

This too is an excellent "starter" before such dishes as those mentioned above. The egg yolk is, as usual, restrained from running around by the embrace of a ring of onion or tomato. If you have no chives to hand you can, here and in most other cases, use chopped spring onions instead or the sprouts of ordinary onions or even chopped onion.

38 4 BONED ANCHOVIES WITH CHOPPED EGG AND CAPERS
Here the chopped, hard-boiled egg is arranged between the parallel rows of anchovy fillets.

39 4 BONED ANCHOVIES WITH SCRAMBLED EGG AND CHIVES
Here, his thoughts far from the House of Davidsen, the proprietor paused in his interpretative wandering through the sandwich list to remark: "Heaven preserve me from cold scrambled egg, particularly if there is flour in it". (See page 92).

40 4 BONED ANCHOVIES IN OYSTER SAUCE
WITH A FRIED EGG ON TOAST
Whenever they think a sandwich or other form of food is not sufficiently substantial, the Danes have a habit of slapping a fried egg on top. As the sandwich should be eaten while the egg is warm ("Heaven preserve anyone from cold fried egg") it is not practical if many of them have to be served.

41 SWEDISH ANCHOVY BIRD'S-NEST
This is a more complicated sandwich than most—and not only on account of its name. In the first place it is one of the few sandwiches which should be served on a *round* piece of bread. (Otherwise: "Don't cut the crust off. Give your teeth some work, not the cook. The birds will get fed anyway"). But who ever saw a square bird's nest? Build a zig-zag wall of anchovies

with strips of beetroot atop them to form the walls of the nest. Place a raw egg yolk in the centre and sprinkle the whole with chopped onion.

42 HOT FRIED EEL

The life history of the eel has already been described inasmuch as it concerns *smørrebrød*. Here it is only necessary to emphasize that the eels must not be too small. They can be dipped in beaten egg and then in a mixture of cracker or biscuit crumbs and flour or in flour alone before being fried in butter or in deep fat.

With fried eel a slice of lemon and a little cucumber salad (recipe on page 101) should be served. Their fresh taste offsets the richness of the eel.

43 HOT FRIED EEL AND REMOULADE

When the Danes sit down to eat eel on occasions when it does not form part of a sandwich they always compete as to who can eat most. Each makes an effort to make a ring of eel bones right around the edge of his plate.

The richness of the eel is harmoniously balanced by the remoulade. Fried eel should always be freshly fried, so freshly that is still quite warm.

44 COD ROE, FRIED

Unless you live somewhere where cod are landed and de-roed (in which case you can boil the roe yourself in salted water) it is easier to use canned roe. Both the Norwegian and Icelandic are excellent. Cut the roe in slices and fry in butter. Alternatively it can be dipped in egg and crumbs or flour. Serve with a twisted slice of lemon.

OPPOSITE: *On the plate: Union Jack Sandwich with caviar and extra garnish (No. 54). On the dish: Roast pork with meat jelly, tomato and pickled cucumber (No. 79). Danablu cheese with grated carrot and raw egg (page 87), Smoked eel and scrambled egg (No. 19), Clipper Sandwich (No. 47).*

45 COD ROE, FRIED, WITH REMOULADE

Toast goes extremely well with cod roe on the basis of the old gastronomic rule that hard and soft make the best combination.

46 COD ROE, FRIED, WITH 2 BONED ANCHOVIES IN OYSTER SAUCE

As *hors d'oeuvres* this has the advantage of being quickly prepared. With this we come to the end of the fish section of the Oskar Davidsen sandwich list. Not believing that the restaurant really could serve all the 177 varieties on the sandwich list, four Americans once ordered one of each. They got them but their faces dropped when they got a bill for Kr. 401 (about $ 55 or £ 20). The visitors took most of their order with them when they left—in a parcel.

Fresh Meats, Poultry, etc.

47 "CLIPPER SANDWICH" (RAW, SCRAPED BEEF, EXPORT CAVIAR AND SMOKED SALMON)

As might be guessed this sandwich represents an aircraft. It was composed in honour of Pan-American Airlines. The caviar is placed on the raw beef in a diagonal stripe (to represent the body of the aircraft). Two strips of smoked salmon, one long and the other short, represent the wings.

48 HANS ANDERSEN'S FAVOURITE (CRISP BACON, TOMATO, LIVERPASTE WITH TRUFFLES, MEAT-JELLY AND HORSERADISH)

This consists of thin, narrow slices of streaky bacon, fried until they are crisp and placed in rows on rye bread. Upon or

between these rows are placed slices of tomato. Upon this a
stripe of liverpaste with truffles and one of meat-jelly recline.
Parallel to these lie freshly cut shavings of horseradish.

It is a fact that in his youth Hans Christian was very fond
of bacon.

49 RARE, SCRAPED BEEF WITH CAPERS, ONIONS AND FRIED EGG

This is really a kind of lightly fried boeuf tartar (see below).
White bread is fried in butter (or toasted) and then spread with
raw, scraped beef. The sandwich is now placed in a pan with
very little butter for just a few seconds, meat-side downwards.

50 BOEUF TARTAR

Research in both the Boston Cook Book and Mrs. Beeton con-
firm that boeuf tartar is probably unknown to most in the
U.S. and the British Commonwealth. According to tradition
the Tartars (Attila, it appears, was one of these) used to keep
raw meat in or under their saddles. Naturally after a day or two
it became quite tender. Boeuf tartar today is raw, *scraped* beef,
placed on the bread with the flat of the knife and then gently
pressed down with the back of the knife in such a manner as to
leave a criss cross pattern of grooves in the meat.

Raw, scraped beef with a raw egg yolk is one of the most
easily digested foods imaginable. Without horseradish, pickles
and capers, you can give raw, scraped meat to a seriously ill
duodenal patient. Ask your doctor!

51 BOEUF TARTAR WITH PICKLES

To eat pickles with beef is a natural thing. But when the beef
is tartar it must be *scraped* and not minced. Even if you put it

through the mincer a dozen times you will not get the same result. And scraping, with a short, sharp knife, allows you to omit the sinews and membranes. The meat, preferably fillet or rump steak, should be young and naturally tender. It must *not* be well hung or it will not taste good when eaten raw. After having been scraped from the piece, the meat should be spread, not too thickly, on buttered, crustless, dry toast or rye bread.

52 BOEUF TARTAR WITH RAW EGG YOLK

This is the classic boeuf tartar in Denmark, prepared as 50 and 51 but with a raw eggyolk in the centre, restrained from roaming around by an onion ring until broken and spread by the guest. The yolk of a hardboiled egg can be used by those who don't like raw eggs. That this sandwich has received a new name is a tribute to American inventiveness (see page 76).

Whether you use the raw or the boiled egg, it should be surrounded by chopped raw onion, capers, and grated horseradish. This *smørrebrød* is popularly known the "Lion Sandwich" and is regarded by the bawdy as suitable food for the newly married.

53 SCRAPED RAW MEAT, SHRIMPS, PARBOILED EGG AND FRESH LETTUCE

This is the first, though not the last, mention of shrimps as a suitable mate for raw beef. "Try dry whisky with this" is the advice given at Davidsen's.

Before leaving caviar it is worth recording that one of the world's greatest delicacies, it is claimed, is raw, scraped beef covered with a thick layer of caviar, preferably Russian though the Danish variety is becoming increasingly popular, especially in the United States.

54 "UNION JACK SANDWICH"

Some people can say it without flowers. Axel Svensson expressed what he felt on May 5, 1945, the day of Denmark's liberation, by composing this sandwich, which is one of the more decorative varieties, in honour of British allies. It is identical with 52 but from the egg to each corner of the bread radiate rows of pink, baby shrimps, each reclining, with arched back, on its tail and shoulders.

55 BOEUF TARTAR WITH TWO BONED ANCHOVIES IN OYSTER SAUCE, EGG YOLK AND CHOPPED ONIONS OR CHIVES

This is for those who prefer some tangy contrast, such as is provided by anchovies, to the raw beef and egg. Otherwise beef tartar needs only coarsely ground black pepper and coarse salt.

This sandwich is designed to tickle your palate and to give you an excuse to enjoy, in a typically Danish manner, an icy *snaps*. If you've no *snaps* within reach any form of hard liquor will serve the purpose!

56 RAW, SCRAPED MEAT, EXPORT CAVIAR AND 2 LIMFJORD OYSTERS FLANKED BY 2 ROWS OF SHRIMPS

This is described as a "luxury sandwich available in the appropriate season". Costing about a dollar, it is one of the most expensive sandwiches on the list. "Russian caviar is best for this *smørrebrød* but black Danish caviar is excellent too."

57 ROAST BEEF WITH TOMATO AND CUCUMBER SALAD

Sirloin of fillet of beef, removed from the bone before roasting, obviously makes the best roast. But other cuts can be used provided they are tender. In Denmark roast beef is always underdone, nowhere raw but brown only on the outside. Although beef takes second place to pork as a Danish national dish, roast beef is surprisingly good, particularly as Denmark does not raise beef cattle.

58 ROAST BEEF WITH CRISP BACON AND ONIONS

To produce crisp bacon is simple—you merely pour off the fat as it emerges from the rashers. Not everyone can produce crisp fried onions. There are several ways of doing so. At Davidsen's they are deep-fried in pure, tasteless and odourless vegetable oil (not fat).

59 ROAST BEEF WITH COLD BÉARNAISE SAUCE

Béarnaise sauce is very popular in Denmark. The real recipe for béarnaise can be found on page 89. A less temperamental substitute can be made by making an ordinary béchamel sauce with milk, butter and flour, mixing with some mayonnaise and adding béarnaise essence to taste.

60 ROAST BEEF WITH SUPERFINE EXPORT CAVIAR

This is a combination even more surprising than caviar on raw beef. But there is a substantial demand for this sandwich just the same.

61 ROAST BEEF AND HORSERADISH

You seldom see a piece of cold beef in Denmark without thin shavings of horseradish.

62 ROAST BEEF WITH REMOULADE

As has been remarked before, the Danes' short cut to remoulade is to take pickles in mustard sauce and chop them finely.

They then mix with a not-too-thick mayonnaise. Finely chopped gherkin, capers and parsley may also be added.

63 ROAST BEEF WITH POTATO SALAD AND CHIVES

Here the potato salad is not the normal Danish one but the international one with mayonnaise or salad cream.

64 FRIED CALF'S LIVER AND ONIONS

The liver is cut thin and dipped in seasoned flour. To make sure that it does not get dry inside, fry it in butter (or other fatstuff) which is not too hot.

65 FRIED CALF'S LIVER WITH FRIED EGG

Here we have a fried egg making a more substantial thing out of a round of bread piled with liver which is just as excellent if it comes from a lamb instead of a calf.

To fry an egg without burning it at the edges is an art. Not too much butter in the pan and not too much heat is the secret. Naturally fried eggs must be served before they grow cold.

66 FRIED CALF'S LIVER WITH CUCUMBER SALAD

Here you have the choice of making the cucumber salad according to the recipe on page 101 or of buying it readymade (see page 108).

A sprinkling of finely chopped parsley on the cucumber salad makes it look and taste more interesting.

67 FRIED CALF'S LIVER WITH BACON AND MUSHROOMS

The button mushrooms are sliced and then fried in butter (no Dane will believe that they could possibly taste better if fried in bacon fat). Add a little coarsely ground pepper. Salt is not necessary.

68 FRIED CALF'S LIVER WITH BACON AND ONIONS

Here Britain's traditional liver and bacon has been combined with Denmark's liver and onions in order to please all comers. Strangely enough smoked bacon is not a traditional Danish dish. Only during recent years have the Danes been inclined to supplement their own fat, streaky pork with bacon. Even so the only smoked bacon available in the Danish shops is thin, streaky rashers.

69 BOEUF MODERNE

is the name recently given to this substantial sandwich which consists of slices of juicy steak, parboiled egg (6—7 minutes), crisp onions and sliced tomato served on Danish sour bread or toast.

70 STEAK AND FRIED ONIONS

This is the classic way of serving beef. The steak is cut in slices before being placed on the buttered bread. This sandwich and those with roast pork are the most popular in Danish restaurants.

71 STEAK WITH FRIED EGG

Here once more we have the idea that half a dozen slices of steak are not enough to make a really substantial sandwich with the result that the steak is topped with a fried egg.

For those who do not share the taste of the Danes for fried eggs on all possible or impossible occasions scrambled egg is suggested as an alternative in this case. Shavings of horseradish and chopped chives should then be added.

72 ROAST DUCK WITH RED CABBAGE AND CUCUMBER SALAD

The Davidsen way to cook a duck so that it will not become dry is to rub salt into it and then to place it breast down for the first half hour of roasting. It should be basted with its own fat. To those who would follow the Danish custom of placing water in the roasting tin, a warning: Not too much water. The classical Danish stuffing for roast duck consists of apples and prunes. With both duck and pork red cabbage is served. The recipe for this is given on page 90 but details of an excellent bottled Danish red cabbage are given on page 109. The experts say that chopped apples and celeriac in a light mayonnaise are no bad idea as an accompaniment to roast duck. "To experience duck at its best place slices of the breast on a piece of really fine bread, spread with duck fat and sprinkle with coarse salt".

73 BRISKET OF BEEF, FRESHLY BOILED, AND HORSERADISH

To satisfy the Davidsen chef the brisket must be heifer meat. In any case it must be young and light in colour. It is best eaten with finely shaved horseradish and coarse salt.

74 BRISKET OF BEEF AND PICKLES

This is the classical Danish way of serving boiled brisket. Naturally the pickles (or piccalilli) chosen are of the greatest

importance. You can't beat the English varieties. Even the Danes admit this.

75 BRISKET OF BEEF AND REMOULADE
In this case the remoulade may by all means taste of tangy ingredients such as finely chopped gherkin or capers.

76 BRISKET OF BEEF WITH TOMATO AND 2 ANCHOVIES
At Davidsen's you will be told, if you ask, that: "The tomato provides the meat with a little juice and the anchovies, which go particularly well with tomato, give the beef a slightly salty taste which makes the mouth water as you eat the sandwich".

77 ROAST CHICKEN WITH CUCUMBER AND TOMATO
With food becoming more international every year maybe the Danes will someday adopt thyme as well as parsley as an accompaniment to roast chicken. And maybe other nations will adopt the meat jelly (recipe on page 98) which makes this particular sandwich something really special.

78 ROAST PORK AND BEETROOT
Pork is Denmark's national meat and this is the Danes' favourite sandwich. "There must be crackling (rind) on roast pork and the crackling must have blisters". The blisters should come of their own accord during the basting if there is no water (or very little if the Danish method of roasting is used) in the baking tin. When the rind has been scored with a sharp knife, pieces of bayleaf, whole cloves and bits of onion are stuck between the strips of rind before roasting.

The Danes, who should know, regard the fresh ham as the

3

OPPOSITE: *Hans Andersen's Favourite (No. 48)*.

best cut for roasting. The whole ham should not weigh more than 11-12 lbs.

79 ROAST PORK WITH TOMATO AND GHERKIN

In most Danish homes there would be some red cabbage left over from the time the roast pork was served hot and this would be placed atop the next day's pork sandwiches.

The Danes also garnish pork with the apple and prune stuffing which often goes with the roast. In summer fresh cucumber salad can be used instead of the gherkin.

80 ROAST PORK WITH MEAT JELLY AND SMOKED HAM

This is a real discovery. First the roast pork, then the meat jelly (see page 98) finally a slice of mild-smoked, sugar-salted ham. Any form of garnish is quite unnecessary.

81 HALF YOUNG PIGEON AND STEWED MUSHROOMS

Not even a Davidsen can satisfactorily explain what a half pigeon is doing on a sandwich. If the pigeon has not been boned the guest will have to remove it from the bread and perform the operation himself, thus defeating the entire idea of the open sandwich.

It is claimed that pigeon with bones is juicier than pigeon without. In any case the pigeon should be served just as it becomes airworthy.

82 LIVERPASTE WITH TRUFFLES, 2 ANCHOVIES
IN OYSTER SAUCE AND FRIED EGG

Given a really good liverpaste (see how to make same on page 96), the most important thing to remember when using it for *smørrebrød* is to cut it in slices rather than to *spread* it on the bread. Anchovies are often used in the making of liver-paste. The latter is so rich that the addition of a fried egg might be expected to frighten even a Danish palate.

To some extent the anchovies neutralise the richness of the egg.

83 LIVERPASTE AND CUCUMBER SALAD

This is a sandwich made daily in many thousands of Danish homes during the months when cucumber is available. At other times of the year pickled cucumber (*asie*, see page 90, gherkins see page 93) or strips of beetroot are used for this simplest of all Danish *smørrebrød*.

84 LIVERPASTE WITH THIN SLICES OF CRISP BACON AND STEWED MUSHROOMS

Mushrooms go well with both bacon and liverpaste. Those who do not want to make mushrooms à la crème, or fear to do so for the sake of their figures, can fry them, whole if they are small otherwise sliced, in the bacon fat. Or console them-selves with the thought that there are even more calories in liverpaste.

85 THE VET'S MIDNIGHT SNACK

This has proved most popular of all the Davidsen sandwich specialities. The original recipe calls for buttered rye bread, a slice of liverpaste spread with goose or duck fat or fat from roast pork, meat jelly and then thin slices of salt veal. The sandwich was taken up by Davidsens at the suggestion of a genuine veterinarian. Nearly every Danish restaurant now lists it. For the culinary genius it is perhaps a pity that such inventions cannot be made copyright but for the good of mankind it is better that they cannot.

86 LIVERPASTE WITH 2 BONED ANCHOVIES IN OYSTER SAUCE AND GRATED HORSERADISH

The liverpaste theme can be varied in many ways. It can be garnished with caviar, finely chopped ox-tongue, curry salad (see page 101), even, according to the experts, with Roquefort cheese and preserved strawberries!

87 LIVERPASTE WITH RUSSIAN HERRING SALAD

The main ingredient of this herring salad is beetroot. Also present are herring, meat, cucumber, Worcester sauce and mustard.

88 LIVERPASTE, SLICED TOMATO AND CUCUMBER SALAD

If this seems too simple what of liverpaste with the breast of a young, just-able-to-fly pigeon with either mushrooms and bacon or just one of the latter two?

89 LAMB'S LIVER, FRIED TOMATO AND MUSHROOMS

This is the only mention you will find of lamb on the O. D. sandwich list. In Denmark few eat lamb except at Whitsun when it is very young, very expensive and quite tasteless. It is then eaten with the ubiquitous cucumber salad.

90 FRIED MEATBALLS AND CUCUMBER SALAD

These meatballs, *frikadeller* as the Danes call them, are another national dish found on every Danish table at least once a week. It is almost true to say that every housewife has her own recipe or method of making *frikadeller*. Even the kinds of meat used vary. Oskar Davidsen's own recipe and another can be found on page 97.

91 FRIED MEATBALLS WITH RED CABBAGE, MEAT JELLY AND BEETROOT

The classical Danish way of serving *frikadeller* is with red cabbage (recipe page 90, where to buy in glasses page 109). For meat jelly see page 98.

92 FRIED MEATBALLS WITH MEAT JELLY AND THINLY SLICED, JUICY SALT VEAL

"Simple things should sometimes be raised to a higher plane. The natural aroma and taste of simple, clean-tasting ingredients should not always be overpowered by over-tangy garnishes."

93 HAM, SLICED EGG AND MEAT JELLY

Denmark is justly famed for her hams of which she has a large export, particularly to the United States. A prime Danish ham should not weigh more than about 12 lbs.

94 HAM AND MEAT JELLY

Though the combination of ham and egg, even hardboiled, is no Danish invention, the addition of meat jelly in this and the previous sandwich really does do things to the palate.

95 HAM AND SCRAMBLED EGG

This is the commonest way of serving ham in Copenhagen restaurants. After tasting the strips of rubbery *æggestand* often served it is not surprising that the Danes themselves sometimes admit that the combination is not exciting. But with real scrambled egg, undiluted wih either milk or water nor yet insulted with flour, the combination (especially if the egg be warm) can be excellent.

96 HAM WITH CAMEMBERT, RAW EGG YOLK AND CHIVES

Other people in other countries have in recent years combined ham and cheese, both hot and cold, with considerable success. Usually the cheese is of the Swiss type but the use in this sandwich of the softer Danish Camembert with the characteristically fine taste is one of Oskar Davidsen's more notable gastronomic discoveries. It is hardly surprising that it makes a special appeal to foreign visitors. The raw egg yolk can, if preferred, be replaced by slices of hardboiled egg.

97 HAM WITH CHICKEN SALAD

It is hardly surprising that so many prefer this to a club sandwich. A recipe for chicken salad can be found on page 101.

98 HAM WITH BOMBAY CURRY SALAD

Here again we have something very special—a combination of cool, mild ham and spicy curry-mayonnaise, the latter here containing macaroni, chicken and giblets.

99 HAM WITH VEGETABLE SALAD

The fine fresh taste of this vegetable salad is obtained by combining chopped beetroot with chopped apple and a little chopped gherkin. To this small peas and mayonnaise are added.

100 HAM WITH FRIED EGG

Even at Davidsen's you can't go far without falling over a fried egg. And just as long as the Danes regard the addition of such as synonymous with extravagance eggs will be dumped

on the top of sandwiches. But the Davidsen fried egg disappears
from the sandwich if it is not to be served on the premises for
a cold fried egg is an abomination of the civilised palate.

101 HAM WITH FRIED CALF'S KIDNEY AND REMOULADE

If the kidney is, as it should be, from a sucking calf, the Danish
custom is to fry and serve it with its fat still attached.

102 HAM WITH BIRDS' LIVER AND FRIED EGG

The birds' liver comes from fowl, chicken or duck as available
and should be sliced. It will be sautéed in a little butter,
pepper and salt being added. And here's that egg again.

A few mushrooms are an extra luxury.

103 HAM WITH HOMEMADE GOOSE LIVERPASTE
AND MADEIRA JELLY

The Davidsen recipe for goose liverpaste is given on page 95
but those who have no goose to hand nor time to spare can
always use Strasbourg gooseliver with equally fine results.
Madeira jelly is ordinary meat jelly (see page 98) to which
Madeira has been added.

104 BAYONNE HAM, ROAST BEEF AND MADEIRA JELLY

"This combination is good", they tell you modestly at Davidsen's. What a triumph of understatement! Doubtless someone
ate ham and roast beef in one and the same mouthful before
this sandwich was first served at Aaboulevard 56. But no doubt
that person selfishly kept the discovery secret. Otherwise people
would be eating beef with ham from Alaska to the banks of the

Limpopo. Anyway it took Danish genius to add the Madeira jelly and present the result on the Oskar Davidsen sandwich list. A favourite with Americans this.

105 CRISP BACON AND FRIED EGG

Here at last, provided it is warm, we have the fried egg justifying its position as part of an open sandwich.

106 CRISP BACON WITH TOMATO AND CAMEMBERT CHEESE

Here we have Danish Camembert combining with bacon as an alternative to ham. The tomato is fresh and sliced, not fried with the bacon.

107 CRISP BACON WITH FRIED ONIONS

As has been remarked earlier smoked bacon is not really native to Denmark. The Danish equivalent is fresh, streaky pork (also known as green bacon). This, fried crisp, is invariably accompanied by fried onions and often by apple sauce too. The onions should be crisp and the way to get them so is to deepfry them in oil.

Here the experts insist that rye bread should be used and not wheaten.

108 CRISP BACON WITH CREAMED MUSHROOMS

Nothing suits mushrooms better than bacon. If only the Danes could be persuaded that mushrooms never taste better than when cooked in bacon fat, maybe they would save on their butter bills.

OPPOSITE: *On the plate: Plaice with luxury garnish (No. 24)*
On the dish: Parboiled egg and caviar (No. 138)
Shrimps, pyramid portion (No. 5), Lobster mayonnaise (No. 13)
Salmon with aspargus and spinach (page 73)
Herring in Heering (page 93)

109 JUICY, TENDER SALT VEAL AND MEAT JELLY

This is another Danish speciality. The meat should be silver-side and if it comes from a heifer it will be better than from a calf. For how to salt veal see page 103. Salt veal must be cut very thin—so thin that it is hardly possible to cut it without a machine. This sandwich is best with white bread spread with spiced dripping or simple bacon fat. The jelly is placed between the bread and the meat.

110 BOILED TONGUE WITH MEAT JELLY

The tongue should come from an ox as calf's tongue has not the same taste and pig's tongue just isn't good enough.

111 TONGUE WITH ITALIAN SALAD

This is the most usual way of serving tongue in Danish restaurants. The Italian salad is described on page 102.

112 TONGUE WITH FRIED EGG

"To elevate a Danish sandwich from the mundane to the luxurious place one fried egg on top."

113 TONGUE WITH HOMEMADE GOOSE LIVERPASTE

If you have a gooseliver on your hands turn to page 95 for the recipe.

114 TONGUE WITH SLICED EGG AND MEAT JELLY

Here we have another excellent combination in which tongue replaces the ham used in No. 93.

115 HOMEMADE COLLARED PORK

Whether the Danish *rullepølse* becomes "collared" this or
that in English or whether it is translated as "pressed" something or other, it can be made of beef, veal, lamb or pork.
In practice it is nearly always made of pigmeat. Perhaps the
best *rullepølse* is made of lamb. In which case the Danes
always roll some parsley in the meat. Many prefer collared
beef to the other three. As can be seen from the recipes on
page 104 these collared meats are usually seasoned with allspice
in addition to pepper and salt. Moreover most of the experts
usually have a pet spice or herb to give the meat a characteristic taste.

116 HOMEMADE COLLARED PORK WITH
SPICED LARD AND MEAT JELLY

No Dane would think of eating collared pork on bread spread
with butter but the addition of the usual delicious (and it
must be delicious or it is frightful) meat jelly is a definite asset.

117 CORNED BRISKET OF BEEF WITH HORSERADISH

This, in all its simplicity, is one of Denmark's most manly open
sandwiches.

Chopped chives can be used instead of horseradish. With
fresh, boiled brisket piccalilli is a frequent garnish.

118 CORNED BRISKET OF BEEF WITH
SPICED LARD AND MEAT JELLY

This is really a variation of No. 109. Which is the better is a
matter of choice. Maybe the brisket has more taste. Celery
salt goes well with corned brisket.

**_119_ CORNED BRISKET OF BEEF WITH
POTATO SALAD AND CHIVES**

The potato salad is the mayonnaise variety and chopped spring
onion or onion sprouts can be used instead of chives if the latter
are not available.

_120_ THE VET'S BREAKFAST

This Oskar Davidsen composition came into being in order
that the veterinarian who was the hero of No. 85 could also
have a bite when he got home after, maybe, bringing a calf
or two into the world during the night. The sandwich consists
of bread spread with spiced dripping on which a slice of liverpaste has been placed. On this meat jelly is arranged and over
the whole are draped thin slices cut from a broad salami.

**_121_ SALAMI WITH RAW EGG YOLK, GRATED
HORSERADISH AND CHOPPED CHIVES**

Another excellent combination in which slices of hardboiled
egg can replace the raw egg.

_122_ SALAMI SAUSAGE WITH MEAT JELLY

Not only one of the simplest and cheapest sandwiches on the
list but a firm favourite with many.

_123_ SALAMI WITH SCRAMBLED EGG AND CHIVES

This is the routine as before, most recently in No. 95.

_124_ SALAMI AND FRIED EGG ON TOAST

Toast is good with many of the sandwiches on this list. With
almost any, in fact, if the _pålæg_ is soft or mainly soft.

125 SALAMI WITH SPICED LARD, SLICED POTATO AND CHIVES

Many may prefer this to walnut bread spread with honey, topped with layers of smoked salmon and caviar and crowned with a half lobster, a bevy of shrimps and three maiden oysters! Potato salad can be used instead of sliced potato.

126 LUNCHEON SAUSAGE WITH MEAT JELLY

Pork luncheon sausage ranks second only to liverpaste as that form of *pålæg* most frequently used in Danish homes. Some boast that they eat it, with never flagging gusto, almost daily. For choice too. Certainly meat jelly can turn the humblest piece of meat, be it veal, beef or pork, into a near-banquet.

Eggs, Salads, etc.

127 ITALIAN SALAD

In Denmark the salad which is called Italian is that which is elsewhere called Russian salad while Dano-Russian salad, even when it is not a herring salad, is something quite different. Dano-Italian salad means mayonnaise + macaroni + diced boiled carrot and peas.

128 BOMBAY TOAST

This tasty snack consists of Bombay curry with hardboiled egg and strips of smoked salmon. The Bombay curry consists of macaroni, chicken meat and giblets in curry-mayonnaise.

129 RUSSIAN HERRING SALAD

Cook a little flour in melted butter without browning. To this add a little yellow mustard powder, some Worcester sauce and some malt vinegar. In this place thin strips of whatever meat happens to be handy, beetroot to give the salad its Russian colour, strips of gherkin, apple and pickled herring. Mix, allow to stand and the result is Russian herring salad.

130 RUSSIAN HERRING SALAD WITH EGG

No herring salad seems complete in Denmark without slices of hardboiled egg.

Almost better is to chop the hard egg and draw a stripe of this diagonally across the *smørrebrød*.

131 VEGETABLE SALAD

What this means to the Davidsen guest is discussed under No. 99.

132 CURRY SALAD

This, which should not be confused with Bombay curry salad, consists of mayonnaise + curry + hardboiled egg + small pieces of meat + asparagus + fingernail-sized pieces of firm tomato. On the bread, yet beneath the salad, a pickled herring tit-bit *(gaffelbidder)* is placed between two slices of hardboiled egg.

133 HOT SCRAMBLED EGG WITH SMOKED SALMON ON TOAST

This would appear to be a better bet than No. 9. This is one of those occasions when, if you want to prevent the heat of the scrambled egg from melting the butter on the toast you can put slices of tomato between toast and scrambled egg.

134 HOT SCRAMBLED EGG, 4 BONED ANCHOVIES IN OYSTER SAUCE AND CHOPPED CHIVES ON TOAST

This variation of the ever-popular scrambled eggs on toast has, strictly speaking, little to do with *smørrebrød*. Nor for that matter has any hot food. But the boned anchovies which make this into a Scotch Woodcock are nicely complemented by the chives.

135 HOT SCRAMBLED EGGS AND FRIED MUSHROOMS ON TOAST

This pleasant snack is another which is really out of place on a *smørrebrød* list.

But it does serve a purpose for it is an excellent starter to a meal at which wine, rather than aquavit and beer, is to be drunk.

136 PARBOILED EGG WITH SHRIMPS

Here we start on the most extensive section of the Davidsen sandwich list. There are no less than 15 sandwiches in this section, plus others already mentioned, which involve parboiled eggs.

137 PARBOILED EGG WITH REMOULADE

Here perhaps it is worth recalling that a parboiled egg at Davidsen's is one which has been boiled for 6–7 minutes according to size. It will then have a firm white but the yolk, though set, will still be moist and not dry and powdery as that of a hardboiled egg. Remoulade is discussed on pages 97 and 100.

138 PARBOILED EGG WITH EXPORT CAVIAR

In case you have forgotten, or never knew, export caviar is the roe of a repulsive looking object called the lumpfish.

139 PARBOILED EGG WITH SMOKED EEL

Here we continue with what we may call "ideas and variations".

Egg, prepared in almost any way, can be successfully mated with almost any other form of *pålæg* on a Danish open sandwich.

140 PARBOILED EGG WITH CHIVES

The Danes have chives even in the winter. A few in a flowerpot and you can have your chives in the kitchen window. Sown in the garden as a border they come up each spring and their blossom can be combined with other cut flowers in a vase.

141 PARBOILED EGG WITH SMOKED SALMON

A strip or two of smoked salmon introduces an air of gaiety and extravagance to the most mundane varieties of foodstuff.

142 PARBOILED EGG AND MEAT JELLY

Once again we have meat jelly lending enchantment to one of the humbler forms of *pålæg*.

143 PARBOILED EGG WITH RUSSIAN HERRING SALAD

The ingredients to be expected in this salad are described under No. 129.

144 PARBOILED EGG AND HERRING TIT-BITS

The tit-bits are still the delicious *gaffelbidder*.

145 PARBOILED EGG AND BONED ANCHOVIES IN OYSTER SAUCE

For where to get canned *gaffelbidder* etc. see page 108.

146 PARBOILED EGG AND PICKLES

Still the possibilities are not exhausted. Maybe they are inexhaustible. Try your own hand. The first thing that comes into your head. Parboiled egg with strawberry jam? And why not?

147 PARBOILED EGG WITH TOMATO AND 2 BONED ANCHOVIES IN OYSTER SAUCE

Hard or parboiled egg with a slice of raw tomato is a favourite summer sandwich in Denmark. And a healthy one too.

148 PARBOILED EGG WITH TOMATO AND FRIED ONIONS

The tomato is sliced and if the onions do not appeal chives can always be used instead.

149 PARBOILED EGG WITH CHEESE MAYONNAISE AND CHOPPED RADISHES

Cheese mayonnaise involves the addition of any not-too-mild grated cheese to the basic mayonnaise on page 96.

150 POACHED EGG ON TOAST WITH STEWED MUSHROOMS AND LOBSTER

This is the kind of thing a Dane means when he talks about "high" sandwiches. The "high" is in the vertical sense—piled high. This is the one and only time a poached egg appears on the famous sandwich list. The lobster is the meat of a half-lobster which explains why it is the most expensive sandwich listed. Many foreigners would probably prefer the ingredients as three separate courses.

151 PARBOILED EGG, TOMATO AND HORSERADISH

Here, almost as an afterthought, we return to the parboiled egg and tomato, this time with horseradish deputising for the fried onions of No. 148.

152 SLICED TOMATO, SCRAMBLED EGG, BONED ANCHOVIES IN OYSTER SAUCE AND CHIVES

Here we enter the vegetable kingdom and the egg appears as second fiddle to the tomato. All the ingredients are old friends.

153 TOMATO AND HORSERADISH

With these old pals, previously used only as a garnish for something more substantial, we come to a series which is claimed not only to be of low calory content but also to be abundant in vitamins.

154 TOMATO WITH SCRAMBLED EGG AND CHIVES

Simple, fresh-tasting yet savoury. Easy on both pocket and waistline.

4

OPPOSITE: *On the plate: Sardine in oil (No. 25). On the dish:*
Salami with potato salad (No. 125),
Roast beef and remoulade (No. 62), smoked venison.

155 TOMATO AND TWO BONED ANCHOVIES IN OYSTER SAUCE

Tomato slices can be combined with almost any other ingredient and anchovies with most.

156 TOMATO AND CRISP FRIED ONIONS

Tomato slices and chopped raw onion is more usual. Chives are good too.

157 TOMATO WITH CHEESE-MAYONNAISE

Cheese mayonnaise is explained under No. 149.

158 TOMATO, FRIED ONIONS AND FRIED EGG

Here, as nobody seems to have thought of putting one on cheese, is the fried egg for the very last time.

159 TOMATO, SCRAMBLED EGG, 2 BONED ANCHOVIES IN OYSTER SAUCE

Here, for the penultimate time, we have that famous oyster sauce.

160 TOMATO, I RAW EGG YOLK, CAPERS, HORSERADISH AND RAW ONION

For any vegetarian who is not a fanatic this would be a banquet.

161 GRATED CARROT WITH RAW EGG YOLK AND SLICES OF LEMON

This, as any Dane will tell you, is children's *smørrebrød*. Otherwise, it seems, the little blighters really go to town on the shrimps when they visit the House of Davidsen.

Cheese

162 CAMEMBERT WITH THIN, JUICY SLICES OF SALT VEAL AND MEAT JELLY

Here this delicate, luscious cheese is again blissfully wed to meat. First a couple of slices of the cheese, then the tasty meat jelly and finally paper-thin slices of salt veal.

163 DANISH EMMENTHAL

Whether or not the Danish cheese can measure itself with the Swiss cheese from which it gets its name must be left to the individual to decide. Both are very fine cheeses, the best in their class and maybe the best of all.

164 SAMSOE

Though this Danish cheese, which is also Swiss inspired, is not quite as nutty as Emmenthal it is the cheese of which most is exported (mainly to Italy, Germany and Britain).

165 MARIBO

is a Dutch-inspired Danish cheese of which up to 4000 tons have been exported in a year. Normally mild-tasting, it can have quite a kick after being stored.

166 OLD HOLSTEINER WITH BUTTER OR SPICED LARD

Though its dry, varigated appearance is against it, this cheese is popular with those who demand cheese with a real kick. This is about the only Danish cheese which is almost better with spiced lard than with butter.

Many Danes like a little meat jelly with Old Holstein cheese.

4*

As with all strong cheeses, this should be cut thinly. Mild
cheese should be cut thick. Strong cheese calls for beer and
aquavit; mild cheese prefers red wine.

167 OLD HOLSTEINER WITH RED CURRANT JELLY

An excellent combination this, the jelly taking some of the
edge off the bite of the cheese. There is no export of this cheese.

168 SMOKED CHEESE WITH FRESH CUCUMBER AND PAPRIKA

The soft smoked cheese which comes from the island of Funen
has a very distinctive and pleasing flavour. It is not exported.

169 CHRISTIAN IX

This can be most easily, though not entirely accurately, described as a Samsoe cheese with caraway seed in it. It is not
exported.

170 DANABLU

Until 1952 this cheese was known as Roquefort although the
French cheese is made from sheep's milk and the Danish from
cow's milk. Naturally the cheeses taste quite different. Which
is the better is a matter of opinion. Abroad this is Denmark's
second most popular cheese.

171 DANABLU WITH A RAW EGG YOLK

In the Danish edition of the Oskar Davidsen sandwich list
this piece of *smørrebrød* has taken, "as a tribute to Swedish
friends", its name from the Stockholm restaurant "Gyllene
Freden". Danablu is sometimes known as "Danish Blue".

172 SMOKED CHEESE WITH RAW EGG YOLK AND CHIVES

Here we have the same smoked cheese as in No. 168 combined
with the raw egg which Davidsen's have made so popular with
smoked herrings, raw steak and blue cheese.

173 POTKÄSE

This is a homemade cheese speciality made from odds and
ends of cheese pounded with rum or brandy in an earthenware
pot. See page 90.

174 POTKÄSE WITH A RAW EGG YOLK AND CHOPPED RADISHES

Though this cheese mixture is not, for obvious reasons, exported,
you can easily make it for yourself. Recipe on page 90.

175 CAMEMBERT

This fine Danish cheese, which we have already enjoyed, in
thought at least, as an accompaniment to bacon and ham,
now stands alone. A luxury cheese with a taste quite distinct
from its French namesake, it is seldom found outside Denmark.

Camembert is the one Danish cheese which should always be
eaten on toast.

176 CAMEMBERT WITH 2 BONED ANCHOVIES
IN OYSTER SAUCE

And here, luxuriously wallowing in oyster sauce (the percentage
of oysters in the sauce is not great, a manufacturer confides)
we prepare to take leave of the famous 4-foot long sandwich
list.

177 I SLICE OF BREAD WITH BUTTER OR DRIPPING

Maybe this is listed for the benefit of the visitor who has already acquired dyspepsia in his native country or maybe in acknowledgment of the fact that the Danes have year-by-year been stealthily reducing the ratio between bread and *pålæg* in their sandwiches until, especially at Oskar Davidsen's, it is now seldom possible to find the former and thereby recognise that a hillock of *pålæg* really is a sandwich.

Using your Imagination

When you have read some or all of this book maybe you will not only have whetted your appetite for *smørrebrød*, Denmark's main contribution to world culture, but also have been inspired to do some culinary creation yourself.

The evening, say the Davidsens, is the best time for *smørrebrød* if you are going to make its consumption a social occasion. The same thing applies if you are merely going to try out Danish open sandwiches on your family. The idea here is to relieve the housewife of trouble with the evening meal. And where our old friends the unexpected guests are concerned it is usually towards sundown rather than a high noon that these flourish and multiply.

Where *smørrebrød* is concerned fantasy has no limit. But it is important to remember that it is easiest to do the thing properly from the start. For the simpler the dish the more pains it is necessary to take with it.

It is important to have a good selection of canned goods in the house—simple things like sardines, tunnyfish, salmon and shrimps, for example. Tubes of mayonnaise or horseradish, glasses of gherkins and pickles can come in useful too. Presumably there will always be eggs and cheese around. Of vegetables, tomato and cucumber are possibly the most useful as they combine with other foodstuffs in so many ways. So do cress, lettuce and lemon. Vegetables play an important part, especially for those who wish to retain their figures—no easy matter in Denmark.

Naturally with *smørrebrød* as with other dishes appearance is

very important. Here neatness and colour and imagination play
equally decisive parts.

Another good rule in composing your own open sandwiches
is that hard and soft go together. By this is meant that liverpaste
goes well on toast or crispbread, that a hard sausage tastes best
on new wheat bread rather than on rye bread (though many
Danes would dispute this).

If the best things in life are free, then many of the cheapest
things must indeed rank close to the best. Many a Danish
housewife alone in her kitchen will treat herself to a piece of rye
bread spread with spiced dripping (see page 91) and topped
with nothing more expensive than coarse (it *must* be coarse) salt.
This incidentally is that princess among Sandwich Maidens,
Miss Ida Davidsen's favourite *smørrebrød*. Then there is the
humble but delicious new potato—what could be better than
rye bread with spiced dripping and slices of waxy new potato,
topped maybe with coarse salt? And what can put the finishing
touch to a piece of *smørrebrød* with salami sausage better than a
couple of slices of cold, new potato, sprinkled maybe with a
little chopped chives or spring onion? And the same goes for
open sandwiches in which the main ingredient is roast beef.
While on the subject of inexpensive ingredients the herring with
its manifold possibilities should not be forgotten. Nor should
the fact that mayonnaise can also work miracles with *smørrebrød*.

But this section is designed to get *you* thinking and composing
so no more about potatoes as *pålæg*.

What happens to cod roe in your country? The Danes, at
least, have a way with it (see page 90). The result is "altogether
excellent on *smørrebrød* with a slice of lemon (squeeze the juice
over the fried roe just before you eat it), with remoulade or
seasoned mayonnaise."

The best garnish for the humble sardine is fresh cucumber

and lemon. It is usually served, reclining on a lettuce leaf, on rye bread. But there is no reason why other kinds of bread, or toast, should not be used.

Fresh cucumber salad or pickles (see pages 101 and 90) is the best garnish for roast meats, according to the Davidsens. Those who prefer fresh cucumber to that soaked in vinegar may like to know that the Danes cut in to the center of the thin cucumber rings and then twist the cut edges in opposite directions so that the pieces of cucumber can stand up on the meat.

A tip worth remembering is that when putting something hot, particularly something such as a fillet of fish (which should always be served hot) or a piece of beefsteak, on *smørrebrød*, you can prevent the butter on the bread from being melted by the heat of the *pålæg* by inserting a lettuce leaf or two, or a couple of thin slices of tomato, between bread and hot *pålæg*.

One of the simplest, and best, kinds of *pålæg* is thinly sliced, crisply fried, streaky bacon. To get it crisp pour off the fat as the bacon yields this. Serve on white bread with either butter or spiced lard. Serve with mustard and finely chopped chives or vegetable salad (see page 103) or sliced raw mushrooms. Liver or kidney, fried in really thin slices, is another most excellent *pålæg*.

Liverpaste, salami sausage and cheese—with these a Danish housewife can cope with any situation. With any of these the Davidsens suggest you should try a Danish *snaps* (see page 105). Cognac is even better, they add, but *eau de vie* is excellent too if the *snaps* bottle isn't handy or as cold as it *must* be when served.

While on the subject of what to drink with improvised *smørrebrød* you may care to know that "even whisky tastes well with *smørrebrød*". No doubt Scotch is meant but there's no reason why you shouldn't experiment with your own favourite distillation. The general question of what to drink with *smørrebrød* is discussed on page 105.

OPPOSITE: *The raw materials of open sandwiches can be anything between Heaven and Earth.*

If you have some variety of pickled herring in the house and it is the season for new potatoes, you have the ingredients of one of the best of Danish snacks: rye bread (crisp bread in an emergency), spread with butter or spiced fat, is covered with slices of cold new potato upon which are placed snippets of pickled herring. The *smørrebrød* is then sprinkled with chopped onion, chives and/or beetroot. A little grated cheese to round things off is no bad idea either.

It is possible to make quite surprising combinations of ingredients on *smørrebrød*, blending fish with meat, meat with cheese, sweet things with savoury things. Few combinations are ever completely original. The traveller in Spanish countries who has eaten *membrillo* (quince jelly) with his cheese or the visitor to Turkey who has preferred to moderate the sweetness of rose petal jam by eating it simultaneously with Adrianople cheese, even the Yorkshireman who eats cheese with his apple pie, will not be surprised to hear a combination of old cheese and quince or strawberry jam recommended.

And while we are experimenting with things which may be new to us what about pickled gherkins on cheese (Swiss type)?

Remember that cheese and all smoked or salt meats must be cut thin when they are to be used as *pålæg*. This is the only guaranteed way to make the mouth water. With regard to slicing things thin, the Danes have the advantage of most other people for they can buy their salt veal or beef, salami or other sausage etc. ready cut. To cut it thin enough without a machine is well nigh impossible. The same applies to rye bread. Every Danish home possesses a guillotine designed to cut slices of rye bread a standard eighth of an inch thick. See photo opposite page 59. To do this by hand is no easy matter.

To cut soft cheese thin, particularly Danish Blue, Roquefort or Gorgonzola, is also difficult—until you know how.

The trouble is that soft cheese sticks to the knife and then breaks or crumbles when you try to remove it. The solution is to cover the blade of the knife with thin paper (tissue paper if this is strong enough). Just fold the paper once and put the blade of the knife in the fold. You will find that the knife cuts the cheese quite as well as if uncovered and that the cheese sticks to the paper instead of to the knife. Lay the cheese on the bread and then peel off the paper carefully.

Many are the celebrities who find their way to Oskar Davidsen's. Sometimes a new sandwich is born in honour of the occasion. Mostly no record is kept of these but research has revealed that the Sam Goldwyn Sandwich consists of crawfish tails with lemon and caviar, that the Temple Fielding Sandwich (of raw beef, shrimps and six oysters) cost a dollar and was the most expensive yet composed and that a Holiday Sandwich, dedicated to the magazine, consists of breast of chicken topped with strips of crisp bacon, slices of fresh cucumber, shrimps, lemon and tomato.

It is seldom possible to invent any completely new combination of ingredients for open sandwiches. At an evening conference when Per Davidsen ordered a piece of rye bread with roast pork garnished with meat jelly and strips of ham for the author, the latter thought that he himself would do some composing and asked for rye bread with ham, garnished with strips of roast beef and Camembert cheese with a sprinkling of paprika. His disappointment on learning that the composition was not new was only tempered by the excellence of both sandwiches, especially the latter!

Invited on one occasion to compose an open sandwich for a funeral Axel Svensson suggested beef with black caviar and horseradish. For a wedding he suggested cold boiled breast of lamb with shrimps but offered no explanation.

Some Homely Sandwiches

BEEF, BRISKET OF

This is best eaten with finely and freshly shaved horseradish and coarse salt. Alternatively it can be served with pickles or piccalilli, with remoulade or with slices of tomato and strips of anchovy as at Davidsen's.

BEEF, ROAST

This too can be served with horseradish and piccalilli. For other combinations see pages 31–32.

BRAWN, PORK

This should be served on rye bread without butter or fat and garnished with beetroot strips. Brawn recipe on page 89.

COD ROE, FRIED

For how to prepare this see page 90. Garnish with a slice of lemon cut to the centre and twisted so that it will stand up.

EGG, HARDBOILED

Slices of egg, boiled for 8 minutes, can be served with strips of anchovy or *gaffelbidder*. Garnished with finely chopped onion, slices of gherkin and capers and decorated with dabs of mayonnaise and cress, the sandwich would be well on its way to becoming a party sandwich.

EGG, PARBOILED

Cut in slices and serve with remoulade. Other parboiled egg combinations will be found on pages 16 and 48–51.

EGG, SCRAMBLED

The Scotch Woodcock is a perfectly legitimate piece of *smørre-brød:* scrambled egg on toast garnished with strips of anchovy. Chopped chives can always be added, so can thin slices of tomato. A slice of ham is placed between the buttered toast and the egg brings this sandwich too into the party sandwich class.

FISHCAKE

Though not the most exciting of things (Danish recipe on page 22), sliced fishcake is at least inexpensive. Serve sliced on rye bread with capers or remoulade.

FISH, FRIED FILLETS

As these should always be warm when served, the buttered rye bread on which they are to be placed should be brought to the table separately or the heat of the fish will melt the butter on the bread. Alternatively use a lettuce leaf to insulate the fish from the bread. Serve with a slice of lemon or with remoulade or both.

HAM, BOILED

Is one of the best of all *pålæg*. The Danes usually top it with a little scrambled egg. Try it with meat jelly or cold new potato. Other combinations are discussed on pages 39–41 and 71.

HAM, SMOKED

This is best served on bread spread with spiced dripping (page 91). A little meat jelly between bread and ham makes the sandwich particularly delicious. Paper-thin back rashers of smoked bacon can be used instead of smoked ham. Sprinkle with chopped chives.

HAMBURGERS, DANISH

Under the name of *hakkebøf* (see page 93), these are a favourite dish in most Danish homes. Served hot with fried onions today they easily become, when sliced, tomorrow's *pålæg*. Garnish with cold fried onions and gherkins or *asie* (see page 93).

HERRINGS, PICKLED

(See page 94). Both spiced and marinated herrings are served on rye (or crisp) bread with chopped onions and capers.

HERRING, SOUSED FRIED

When the Danes have fried herring for dinner mother always fries some extra fish so that these can be soaked in vinegar etc. (see page 94) overnight and thus become *pålæg* the next day. Serve with their onion rings but make sure that the liquid has drained off both herrings and onions as much as possible or the rye bread will become soggy.

LAMB, ROAST

Cold roast lamb, with fresh cucumber or cucumber salad, with meat jelly or mint jelly, with sliced gherkin, chopped dill or piccalilli is an excellent *pålæg*.

LIVER, FRIED

This is best served with a few crisp fried onions or rashers of crisp bacon. See also pages 32–33.

LIVERPASTE

This is the kind of *pålæg* which, after luncheon sausage, is most used in Denmark. And very excellent it usually is. Recipes are legion (see page 96). Most Danes spread the liverpaste, but it tastes better when laid on the bread in slices. Meat jelly is one of the best garnishes for liverpaste, but strips of beetroot, slices of cucumber, cucumber salad or pickled cucumber (*asie*) can also be used. Other sandwiches with liverpaste will be found on pages 36–38 and 72. Canned liverpaste is never quite the same as the freshly-made variety, whether this be homemade or bought at a delicatessen.

LUNCHEON MEAT

is seldom seen in Denmark yet it makes an excellent *pålæg* as does the luncheon sausage (*kødpølse*) so popular among the Danes. Serve in not-too-thin slices with meat jelly and slices of cucumber or gherkin.

MEATBALLS

Danish recipe on page 97. The Danes cut them in slices and serve them on buttered rye bread with red cabbage (page 90) or kind of pickled cucumber or other (page 90).

PORK, BOILED

The Danes often have cold boiled fat pork in the house as this goes with split pea soup, one of their national dishes. It is eaten on rye bread without butter but with strips of beetroot or gherkin.

PORK, FRIED

Striped pork is what the Danes call this popular dish which is eaten both hot and cold with apple sauce and fried onions. The name arises because the pork (sometimes known as green bacon) is streaky (fat alternating with lean). The meat is cut in thick rashers and fried crisp. To get it crisp, pour off the fat as it comes out of the meat. If a little onion, some salt if necessary, and maybe a little thyme is later added to the fat while this is boiled up again, the fat will, when cold, be an excellent spiced dripping for use instead of butter under salt and smoked meats and certain kinds of sausage.

PORK, ROAST

Place thin slices of roast pork on buttered bread and garnish with meat jelly, cucumber salad or sliced gherkin or beetroot or red cabbage. Small pieces of crackling are often added too. If enough is piled on, this sandwich enters the party sandwich group.

PORK, ROAST SPARE RIBS

This, garnished as roast pork above, makes a very special sandwich.

PORK, SMOKED SADDLE OF

This, called *Hamburgerryg* by the Danes and Canadian Style Bacon across the Atlantic, is one of their noteworthiest specialities. In Denmark the saddle of pork from which the *hamburgerryg* is made is only slightly salted and smoked. Used as smoked ham without being boiled it is an excellent *pålæg* which, cut

OPPOSITE: *Salami with potato salad (No. 125),*
Ham with Camembert, raw egg yolk and chives (No. 96),
Roast beef and remoulade (No. 62),
Rolled, pressed sausage or collared pork (No. 116).

thin, and served on bread spread with spiced dripping, can be garnished with chopped chives. After being boiled it also tastes excellent on open sandwiches. (See recipe on page 99).

PORK TENDERLOIN

Cut in not too thick slices and fried, or fried whole and then sliced, these are really in the party sandwich class. Serve with fried onions.

POTATO

Sliced potato, preferably new, on bread spread with bacon fat or spiced lard plus coarse salt and maybe some chopped chives, is about the cheapest and forms one of the best combinations it is possible to use for open sandwiches. Slices of cucumber, cut to the centre and twisted so that they stand up, make this sandwich look festive. New potatoes can also be garnished with anchovy or *gaffelbidder* strips and chopped dill. Slices of tomato can also be used to garnish.

SALAD, COD OR OTHER FISH

An excellent *pålæg* can be made by mixing flakes of cold cod or other boiled fish in a stiff mayonnaise and adding a little tomato ketchup with a good dash of Worcester sauce. A few shrimps sprinkled deceptively on top of the salad make it look more exciting.

SALAD, CURRY

For this see page 101.

SALAD, HERRING

See page 102 for this inexpensive and excellent *pålæg*.

5

SALAD, RUSSIAN HERRING

See pages 46 and 47.

SALAD, ITALIAN

Serve on rye bread, possibly with a lettuce leaf between bread and salad. Decorate with tomato slices and, if liked, cress. Recipe on page 102.

SALAD, MACKEREL

This excellent-tasting salad is easily made by mixing the contents of a tin of mackerel, preferably in tomato sauce, with some mayonnaise. Decorate with cress.

SALAD, TUNA

As with mackerel but using tuna or tunnyfish instead.

SALT VEAL OR BEEF

Place some meat jelly between the bread, which should be spread with spiced dripping, and the thin slices of meat. See recipe on page 103.

SARDINE

This really requires no more than a piece of lemon.

SAUSAGES

Any kind of sausage can be used on open sandwiches: from blood sausage to Bologna and Mortadella and Butifarra or Leverwurst. Most taste better on spiced dripping or bacon fat than on butter. Some good meat jelly improves most of them too.

SAUSAGE, COLD PORK OR FRANKFURTERS

Cut lengthwise, even these can be used as *pålæg*. A little sliced gherkin or beetroot or some fine shavings of horseradish are an excellent garnish.

SAUSAGE, PRESSED ROLLED

This *rullepølse* is one of the most popular varieties of everyday *pålæg*. The recipe is given on page 104. It is eaten on rye bread spread with fat.

TOMATO

Some of the many sandwich possibilities of this fruit will be found on pages 51–52. The most popular of all consists of slices of hardboiled egg with slices of tomato on top or beside them.

TONGUE

Some of the less elaborate ways of serving this are mentioned on page 43.

VEAL, ROAST

Can be served with strips of crisp bacon, meat jelly and strips of gherkin or with asparagus salad. If the veal has been roasted with a stuffing such as thyme and parsley, a little of this makes a fine garnish.

Some Party Sandwiches

CHICKEN BREAST, BOILED

with slices of tomato or asparagus or even horseradish salad with whipped cream.

CHICKEN BREAST, BOILED OR ROAST

with mayonnaise and slices of tomato is as good and straightforward as any upper class sandwich. It can also be served with bacon and mushrooms, with vegetable salad, with shrimp salad, or with meat jelly (chicken jelly maybe), tomato and cucumber slices.

EEL, FRIED

is not regarded as a delicacy by most Britons and Americans. But the Danes regard eel, especially the smoked variety, as one of their greatest and most festive delicacies. Certainly the many calories which eels contain help the Danes, maybe the eels too, to keep out the cold during the winter. Fried eel (see recipe on page 91) really requires no further garnish than a slice of lemon cut to the centre and twisted so as to sit astride the eel. Serve on rye bread or toast with a stripe of scrambled egg parallel with the pieces of eel and garnish with chopped chives.

EEL, JELLIED

is a very popular dish in Scandinavia. A recipe appears on page 92.

EEL, SMOKED

The life story of the eel has been written on page 19. There is a great difference in taste between canned smoked eel and the freshly smoked variety. Axel Svensson suggests that you don't let the family see the eel until it appears, cut in pieces, on the table. Use rye bread, if possible, otherwise toast. It is difficult to imagine smoked eel on white bread.

GOOSE BREAST, SMOKED

makes excellent *pålæg*. Scrambled egg is a useful garnish. Smoked breast of turkey is almost better.

GOOSE LIVERPASTE

either canned or made according to the recipe on page 95, is best served on toast.

HAM, BOILED

If you can find a really good loaf of wheat bread, some fine butter and a really distinguished ham, then you have an unbeatable combination. But remember not to permit any other disturbing taste to be superimposed. If you are going to combine anything with ham, nothing is better than a good liverpaste. Here Strasbourg *pâté de foie gras* is of course best but several Danish factories produce fine liverpaste with truffles.

HAM, SMOKED

While most Danes would eat this on bread spread with spiced dripping and garnished with nothing more than chopped chives, the experts admit the possibility of using butter and pineapple instead.

KIDNEY AND BACON

is an excellent combination to use on rye bread or toast. It is perhaps most convenient to have the kidney in small pieces. Fried mushrooms are an asset. Any kind of kidney can be used. So can chicken or duck liver. A suitable touch of colour can be provided by a slice of tomato.

LIVERPASTE

As will be seen from the recipe on page 96 anchovies or pickled herring are used in most liverpastes. But for those who like the tangy taste of these fish there is no reason why anchovies or *gaffelbidder* should not be served atop the slices of liverpaste. Some small pieces of beetroot or tomato will add a little colour. Liverpaste and oxtongue go well together—garnish with meat jelly. So does ham—garnish with piccalilli. Or what about liverpaste with slices of crisp bacon and shavings of horseradish? For other liverpaste suggestions see pages 36–38.

MUSSELS, PICKLED

These are generally available both in glasses and cans. They were once on the Davidsen list with remoulade.

MUSSELS, SMOKED

These recently appeared on the Danish market in cans and are most tasty. Garnish with finely grated pickled cucumber mixed with lemon juice. Or with finely grated horseradish and finely chopped lettuce mixed with oil and vinegar dressing.

SALAD, CRAB

This is made in exactly the same way as the lobster salad mentioned on page 102. Serve with a little chopped parsley.

SALAD, CHICKEN

is described on page 101. No garnish is necessary as all the ingredients are in the salad. If you want something extra good include shrimps and truffles or just a sprinkling of "morning-picked, dew-shining parsley which should preferably be chopped with a brightly polished silver knife".

SALAD, LOBSTER

A recipe is on page 102. Crab can also be used.

SALAD, NORWEGIAN HERRING

Serve the fillets of herring (prepared as explained on page 102) on rye bread after letting as much as possible of the marinade run off so that it will not soak into the bread. Garnish with rings of raw onion, capers and slices of tomato cut to the centre and twisted to stand up.

SALAD, SALMON

A recipe for salmon mayonnaise will be found on page 100. Garnish with lobster, shrimps, oysters, mussels, caviar or slices of egg, tomato and cucumber.

SALAD, SHRIMP

prepared the Danish way is mentioned on page 103. There is no better garnish than more shrimps.

SALMON, SMOKED

This should, according to the Davidsens, always be cut thin. Use three thin slices rather than one thick. Most people eat smoked salmon on wheat bread though some prefer rye bread.

Most Danes expect, however, thick bread, butter and salmon. Freshly ground pepper may be used on smoked salmon but never salt. If you want any garnish on the salmon the experts warn against the familiar Danish cress. But you can garnish with scrambled egg and chopped dill or with heads of asparagus with a stripe of spinach. Davidsen's once had an open sandwich consisting of a purée of smoked salmon with raw eggyolk and horseradish. Chopped onion is suggested as an alternative to the horseradish. Some other Davidsen salmon combinations will be found on pages 16 and 17.

SHRIMPS

Just about everything which can be said about shrimps on open sandwiches has been said on page 15. Almost the only possible variation seems to be to use more shrimps. But, as can be seen throughout the Davidsen sandwich list, shrimps can be used as a garnish for many other kinds of sandwich.

SWEETBREADS

Although very seldom encountered on open sandwiches in Denmark, sweetbreads are most suitable as *pålæg*. How to deal with them appears on page 104. As *pålæg* small pieces of sweetbread can be served in a thin mayonnaise dressing to which tomato ketchup or curry powder has been added. In this form they can be garnished with lobster. One can also serve pieces of fried sweetbread with remoulade and maybe mushrooms and cucumber. Tongue too goes well with sweetbreads. The latter should here be served lukewarm in a bowl with green beans. Hand toast and butter.

TARTAR BEEF

Just about all that can be said on this subject will be found on pages 28–29.

TONGUE, OX

There's no getting away from the fact that oxtongue is best. One way of serving it is to roll slices around a little Italian salad, serving three such rolls on each sandwich. Top these with a dab of mayonnaise and a little parsley. Tongue can also be served with remoulade (page 100) and chopped parsley.

TURKEY BREAST, SMOKED

This is a fine *pålæg* but no pineapple, please.

The Poetry of Open Sandwiches

The English language does not lend itself well to songs in praise of gastronomy and even less to gay frivolity on the subject of food. Danish is such a mundane language that one would expect no more of it. The Davidsens have proved the contrary. Not only do they believe that their sandwiches should appeal to the palate but also to the eye and *to the ear*. This has led them to descriptions which have passed into, and enriched, the Danish language.

At Davidsen's you never eat a mere chicken, it is always a "milk-fattened, manor-bred chicken". Pigeons are always "hand-caught Roman pigeons", hand-caught because they were too fat to fly away, and smoked salmon often becomes "silver-glistening, juniper-smoked Bornholm salmon".

Most famous of all are the House of Davidsen's "night-caught, morning-boiled, hand-peeled, coral-pink Kalvehave shrimps". What could sound fresher or more delectable? The best description ever made of shrimps is the name which Axel Svensson gave to sandwich No. 4 on the Davidsen list. And here, as explained below, it took an American to provide a perfect translation for the pile of shrimps known as *"Rejer i trængsel"* —"The Rush Hour".

On Davidsen's sandwich list and menus too you will come across such expressions as "butter-fried", "parsley-sprinkled", "Burgundy-poached" and "Madeira-spiced". And, describing the famous scraped raw beef tartar, "lefthand-scraped". Here the right hand has been overworked doing a super-quick job so that the meat can really live up to its fresh-scraped label.

Something of this poetry of the open sandwich was introduced to New York on March 18, 1955, when the Explorers Club held their annual dinner at the Waldorf Astoria. On this occasion intrepid explorers were presented with a series of what were described as "Cocktail Smorrebrod" designed and prepared by Arnold H. Haverlee. Tribute was paid, in a sandwich card introducing the "smorrebrod", to the fame of Madame Oskar Davidsen who, according to tradition, started the restaurant side of the business which still bears her husband's name. The card then went on to list, with a series of delightful and extremely original English names, details of the *smørrebrød* served. In Copenhagen these were later found to be so good that at least one name was, with grateful thanks to the unknown poet who conceived it, adopted for the English edition of the Oskar Davidsen sandwich list.

The following, taken from the Explorer's Club list, show what can be done, both in the way of terminology and the combination of ingredients for use on *smørrebrød*, beyond the Atlantic:

Gold Miner's Sweetheart. Smoked salmon, scrambled eggs topped with red caviar, chopped onion.

Fairies' Delight. Asparagus tips rolled in ham, sliced hardboiled egg with pansies in aspic. Axel Svensson admitted, when the point had been explained, that he could never have found a more appropriate combination.

Mussels in Bed. Smoked mussels on cream cheese, chopped chives, sliced radish.

Strip Teaser's Special. Scraped raw choice beef, peeled shrimp, raw egg yolk with capers.

Lovers' Tryst. Pressed spiced baby lamb, crisp bacon, violets in wine glaze.

The Hangover. Herring in oyster sauce, raw onion rings.

Middle-Age Spread. Roast fresh ham, peas and carrots in mayonnaise, parsley.

The Rush Hour. Shrimp piled on shrimp, remoulade sauce.

Politician's Promise. Sliced bologna, cheese strip, sour pickle.

Mother-in-Law. Crabmeat salad, marigolds in mayonnaise.

Honeymoon. Raw oyster with horseradish and bacon.

Reading such an inspired menu as this led to the belief that a new parlour game had been born. Trial and much error showed that the game was not so easy. A little thought produced a string of potential sandwich names which appeared to offer possibilities, names such as Pickwick, Guy Fawkes, Lover's Tiff, Once Bitten, Private Secretary, Maiden's Prayer, Billingsgate etc. and a string of amusing ingredients—chicken's liver, sour grapes, bitter almonds, sucking pig, tripe etc. The trouble was to mate the two parts. It was obvious that Old Man's Fancy had to be something to do with lamb or breast of chicken, that Perfidious Albion had to contain roast beef but as far as combinations of name and ingredients were concerned no progress was made beyond The Taming of the Shrew—chicken, tongue and Italian salad. If anyone meets with greater success at this game, the author, c/o his publisher, would be delighted to hear of it and even, with picture books of Denmark at the said publisher's expense, to reward the best suggestions.

Canapés and Cocktail Delicacies

The French word canapé is derived from a Greek word meaning "a couch with mosquito curtains". The English word canopy has a similar origin. Today canapé still means a sofa to the French. But it also means an appetizer consisting of a piece of toast or fried bread topped with anchovies, caviar, shrimps, salmon, lobster or some other delicacy and garnished.

Canapés can be of any shape and are often round. Whether of toast, of fried or fresh white bread or of rye bread, they are invariably crustless and their size is such that they can be eaten in one or two mouthfuls.

Less substantial than full-sized open sandwiches yet more satisfying than mere cocktail delicacies, canapés can be served with drinks before a meal, as the first course of a meal, as a light meal before or after the theatre, as an accompaniment to that last drink before the guests leave and on many another occasion. Certainly they can bring a touch of distinction to a tea table too.

Before elaborating on the subject of canapés it might be as well to establish what is meant by "cocktail delicacies". Inventive people in many countries have given these a number of names. As the Danes say "beloved children have many names". What characterises all these *bonnes bouches* is that they are small enough to be raised to the mouth with the aid of the toothpick, or some plastic substitute for same, with which they are supplied.

Finally come what the Danes call *snitter*. These are half sandwiches. In view of the massive proportions assumed by the modern Danish open sandwich, in restaurants in particular, it is hardly surprising that even such renowned trenchermen as the successors of the Vikings cannot deal with full-scale *smørrebrød* on all occasions. Restaurant guests began to divide the sandwiches they had ordered. This had the added advantage of making it possible for each to have twice as many *different* sandwiches as he would otherwise have been able to cope with. Later restaurants began to serve these half-sandwiches as *snitter*. Now all are prepared to do so, taking (as the matter is not as simple as merely cutting one big sandwich into two) two-thirds of the price for *snitter* as for proper *smørrebrød*. In this way *snitter* have to a considerable extent trespassed on the preserves of canapés.

Oskar Davidsen canapés are mostly served on rounds of buttered white bread. At home these can be stamped out with a wine glass. But rye bread too is used for both canapés and *snitter;* the shape of these varying according to the *pålæg*. For example it is hardly practical to cut roast beef into small round slices and the shape of a smoked herring makes an oblong piece of bread more practical than a round one. On the other hand salads are best on rounds of bread. As can be imagined no mere pastes are used on Davidsen canapés. Nor, on the other hand, are these ever grilled, toasted, topped with pineapple or otherwise abused.

In composing your own canapés and *snitter* you can proceed on the same lines as when marshalling ingredients for fullsized open sandwiches, subject, however, to the limitations imposed on your fantasy by available space. In other words no attempt should be made to pile too many things on a small piece of canapé bread or toast. Two ingredients, or three at the most, will usually be sufficient. To set you thinking here are some suggestions:

BOEUF TARTAR

This way of serving raw beef has been described on page 28. Rye bread or toast is best. If the canapé is to be eaten with the fingers a slice of hardboiled egg yolk will be more practical than a raw egg yolk!

CAVIAR

Toast round, square or triangular pieces of wheat bread and butter when cold. Arrange anchovy fillets on the toast and between them caviar. Decorate with chopped egg yolk and a piece of lemon and serve on a crisp lettuce leaf.

ANCHOVY

Arrange the anchovy fillets on the bread or toast. Alternately between the fillets place chopped white and egg yolk. Decorate with chopped parsley.

CARDINAL

On toast or fried bread place a salad of chopped apples, button mushrooms and gherkins in pink-coloured mayonnaise. Crown with a dab of caviar.

ST. HUBERT

Finely chopped game in its own rich, thick sauce is placed in a ring of paprika butter and garnished with red currant or other jelly.

TONGUE

Spread with French or other mustard and cover with slices of tongue. Decorate with Italian salad (page 102) and cress.

LUCILE

In the centre chopped breast of chicken. Around this chopped tongue. Garnish with mustard butter.

RUSSE

Oval, fried crouton with smoked salmon. Upon this a slice of hardboiled egg crowned with a dab of caviar.

KIEV

Round pieces of toast are covered with black caviar. On this is placed, in a hollow, a raw egg yolk or an oyster.

CHICKEN

Slices of chicken breast on wheat bread with asparagus tips in curry-mayonnaise and a sprinkling of paprika.

SHRIMPS

Shrimps, with or without mayonnaise, on round pieces of wheat bread topped with a snippet of lemon.

Meet the Danish Cheese Family

Since 1945 Danish cheese has been finding its way to more and more markets (the current number is around 90). In less than 10 postwar years the country's cheese production was up to 1,700,000 cwt. and of this, 1,180,000 cwt. was exported. Some indication of the quality of Danish cheese and the respect in which it is held can be gauged from the quantities which are bought by such cheese-producing countries as Italy and Switzerland. After Germany, the United Kingdom is Denmark's best cheese customer. Only import restrictions limit the quantities exported to the United States.

In 1952 Denmark signed an international convention with a number of other cheese-exporting countries to safeguard regional cheese names. Since then 11 Danish cheeses, which had hitherto borne such names as Danish Roquefort, Danish Swiss, Danish Gongonzola, Danish Gouda etc. despite the fact that they had attained characters all their own, were given Danish names. Even today few Danes know the new names and it may well take a generation before they become really familiar with them.

Below the principal Danish cheeses are discussed and some mention is made of their characteristics. *Velbekomme*—"May they become you well"—as this Danish word would have been translated in Shakespeare's days.

SAMSOE, THE GOLDEN,

is a rich, round cheese with a succulent, slightly sweet flavour, reminiscent of golden cornfields and the clean scents of harvest

6

OPPOSITE: *Office lunch: Boiled brisket of beef with horseradish (page 62), Salami, rolled pressed sausage (page 69), Luncheon sausage (page 65), Liverpaste with cucumber (page 65), Cheese with radishes (page 83).*

time. The Danes slice all cheeses of this kind very thin, using special cutters which either function like a wood-plane or consist of a wire closely attached, and parallel to, a metal rod. But to enjoy the delicate flavour of Samsoe to the full it should be cut into fingers. Samsoe cheese is of the gruyère type.

DANBO, THE FESTIVE CHEESE,

is an honoured member of the Samsoe family. Glossy and handsome it not only looks good but tastes good too. Square and solid in character without being hard, this is a cheese to round off a banquet. Mild and friendly, it beams on any distinguished gathering from its small shining holes. Danbo is a cheese of the Steppe type which was once, maybe still is, produced in Russia.

FYNBO, THE GENTLE CHEESE,

is from the Hans Andersen country and like the famous storyteller is a favourite with children. It is rich and soft and has no "bite". Fynbo is a much firmer cheese than its first cousin the Samsoe and slightly smaller, but like the rest of the family is possessed of a rich fragrance. It was inspired by Dutch Gouda.

ELBO, THE FAMILY CHEESE,

is a healthful, nourishing cheese, brick-shaped and with a bright red rind. It is a particularly hard cheese which stores well. Mild yet full flavoured, it is a favourite of women and children. Although a member of the Samsoe family it has fewer holes than its relations.

TYBO, THE AROMATIC,

is slightly smaller than its cousin the Elbo and much less matter-of-fact. Its fine rich aroma, inherited from distinguished ancestors, makes it a very revered member of the Samsoe family. There is a touch of magic about its flavour according to Danish folk lore.

MOLBO, THE HOMELY,

is red, round and yellow when cut. As with the other members of the Samsoe family it is rich and mild and not too soft. The holes are few. The Molbo is a family cheese to be eaten and enjoyed anywhere at any time. Its forebears were Dutchmen from Edam.

MARIBO, THE MASCULINE,

is not a Samsoe cheese but is in the direct line of another noble family. Stronger than Samsoe, it is more stimulating but never fierce. With a pleasantly surprising "after taste", it is a man's cheese—a connoisseur's. In the making it is kneaded and whipped, the air being encouraged to get in as this gives it an acid quality. The Danes say the small holes in the cheese contain the taste! Another Dutch type from Gouda.

HAVARTI, THE FEMININE,

is a light yellow cheese named after a Danish farm from which about 100 years ago the farmer's wife travelled widely to study the mysteries of cheesemaking. The cheese resembles somewhat the Tilsit cheese of southern Russia. When young it tastes fresh and a trifle acid, but as it matures it becomes sharp and more dominating.

ESROM, THE FRAGRANT,

is a mild cheese caressing the most delicate of palates. Packed in tinfoil, it is as pure as it is golden and can be eaten from the rind to the core. Its forefathers came from Port Salut.

6*

DANABLU, THE NOBLE

Milky white with blue blood in its veins describes the qualities of Danish Blue. It ripens very quickly and is whiter and sharper than all other Danish cheeses. It is of the same noble family as Roquefort.

MYCELLA, THE GRATIFYING,

is a mature cousin of Danish Blue, with a cream or olive complexion and green veins instead of blue. The flavour is gentle and mildly aromatic. It will melt ingratiatingly on the tongue when matured just so long as not to be too solid. Its southern complexion reveals its affinity to Gorgonzola.

EMMENTHAL, THE GIANT,

is as large as a cartwheel but mild and sweet. It must be matured for about seven months and when cut will then be firm and white with large holes. It is a luxury cheese in itself and asks nothing more than a piece of fine bread.

CAMEMBERT,

has a flavour which varies according to ripeness. Feel the cheese with the finger, the softer the cheese the stronger and more characteristic the flavour. Danish Camembert is a shining, appetising yellow.

BRIE, THE MILD,

is the larger but thinner sister of the Camembert. It has more crust too, which is delicious eating. Brie is usually milder than Danish Camembert.

Cheese Fantasy

When using really fine cheese for *smørrebrød* most people will prefer not to distract the attention of their palates from the cheese itself. Nevertheless there are certain fruits and vegetables which seem to emphasize the flavour of certain kinds of cheese. Bananas or apples, eaten in alternate mouthfuls with cheese of the Samsoe or Swiss type, are no new discovery. Nor is the combination of chutney, or spring or pickled onions, or pickled walnuts, gherkins, celery or radishes, with cheese. Most of these can also be used to garnish *smørrebrød* with cheese. For jaded palates, however, or those who like to experiment or have less exciting cheeses than Danish to hand, here are some cheese *smørrebrød* recipes. They are a few of the cheese specialities which have appeared on supplementary Oskar Davidsen sandwich lists.

DANISH BLUE

with finely grated raw carrot and a raw egg yolk. Roquefort can also be used.

DANISH BLUE

with apple rings fried in butter and horseradish-mayonnaise.

HOLSTEIN CHEESE

with sliced cucumber and red currant jelly.

SAMSOE WITH DANISH BLUE

the latter mashed with portwine and seasoned with paprika, the whole topped with slices of winter radish.

CREAMED CHEESE

(i. e. a mixture of grated or pounded cheese and butter) with sliced tomato and chives.

PETIT SUISSE

on toast with a diagonal stripe of caviar.

PETIT SUISSE

with apple rings fried in butter.

PETIT SUISSE

with slices of fresh strawberry and a few grains of sugar.

EMMENTHAL CHEESE

with slices of gherkin.

**SAMSOE WITH RAW, SCRAPED BEEF
AND SLICES OF FRESH CUCUMBER**

is one of Davidsen's latest creations. In this rare case the peel should, for the sake of the colour, be left on the cucumber. Scraped beef is described on page 28.

Finally some Danish advice on the subject of cheese:

"A tasty cheese calls for beer and snaps, a mild cheese for red wine".

"For *smørrebrød* cheese should always be cut thin". (See page 60).

"Don't cut off the crust of Camembert cheese because all the vitamin B is in the crust".

Recipes

BEARNAISE SAUCE

This is an easily made recipe for cold Béarnaise sauce which requires no cooking. Take ¼ lb. butter, 2 large egg yolks, ¼ teaspoonful salt, a good tablespoonful each of salad oil and Béarnaise essence, 1 teaspoonful onion juice and ½ teaspoonful parsley. Place the egg yolks, salt and onion juice in a bowl and while beating add salad oil drop by drop. When the mixture has thickened add the Béarnaise essence and chopped parsley. Melt the butter and add to the mixture a teaspoonful at a time, continuing to beat until all the butter has been absorbed. Place on ice until required. For another recipe see page 31.

BRAWN (SYLTE)

The traditional Danish way is to take a pig's head, soak it, scrub well, remove the eyes and ears and boil for four hours with a bayleaf, an onion, some thyme, peppercorns and salt. Infinite patience is now necessary for the process of picking the meat from the bones and cutting it into neat pieces. When this has been done place the meat in a mould or basin with a little allspice between each layer and, if liked, a little grated onion. Cover with some of the liquid in which the head was cooked and place under light pressure until the brawn has jellied.

A less economical but easier method is to buy belly of pork and pork bones. Boil the meat with salt, bayleaf and peppercorns until tender. Boil the bones with the liquid from the meat for several hours. Cut up the meat and continue as for pig's head brawn.

RED CABBAGE

Take a medium-sized red cabbage and shred it finely. Cook gently in a saucepan with a cup of water, ½ cup vinegar, ½ cup of sugar and a teaspoonful salt until tender (about 2 hours). The vinegar in which the beetroot has been standing can be used instead of fresh vinegar. Pour off some of the liquid if it seems too wet. The addition of a ¼ cup of red currant juice or jelly, always done in Denmark, gives a fine flavour.

So does the substitution of red wine for some of the vinegar and the addition of a little grated apple.

POTTED CHEESE (POTKÄSE)

This is an excellent, and tasty, way of using up odds and ends of dry cheese. Grate finely and moisten with port wine. Cover and allow to stand for 24 hours. Add salt and pepper to taste and a little paprika. And, if available a, little rum. Stir well with a little more port, place in a mould and store in a cool place.

FRIED COD ROE

Boil the roe whole for about 10 minutes in water with a little salt and vinegar. Allow to cool, cut carefully into slices and quickly fry a light brown in melted butter. Allow the slices to cool if they are to be used for open sandwiches.

PICKLED CUCUMBERS

These *asier* are large pickling cucumbers. Peel them, cut lengthwise into two halves and remove pith and seeds. Cover with salt and allow to stand for 24 hours. Next day wash and dry thoroughly and place in a container, preferably earthenware.

Pour over boiling vinegar (2 quarts is sufficient for 10 large cucumbers). To each quart of vinegar must be added 1 dessert-spoonful of mustard powder, 1 teaspoonful white pepper, a score or so of peppercorns, 3 chillies, a few sprigs of dill and sugar to taste. (Sufficient sugar must be used or the pickle will not keep —the Danes use 1 lb.–1 ½ lbs. to the quart). Allow to stand for 3 days. Remove the cucumber, bring the vinegar to the boil and simmer for ¼ hour before pouring over the cucumber. When cool, cover and store in a dry place.

SPICED DRIPPING

Melt some refined lard or slowly fry a few slices of fat pork or bacon. In the melted fat fry a little chopped onion and some leaves of thyme without browning. Strain the fat, or not, as you prefer. When cold use on open sandwiches when the *pålæg* is salt or smoked meat (including salami etc.), liverpaste etc. Diced apple may be added with the onion though this reduces the length of time the fat can be stored. Rosemary can be substituted for thyme.

FRIED EEL

No Danish housewife would ever buy a dead eel unless it were a smoked one. Fortunately her fishmonger has tanks for them to swim in until required. To give good-sized pieces for *smørre-brød* the eel should not weigh less than 1 lb. In whatever condi-tion you receive your eel it must be washed, skinned and dried before you can fry it. Divide into pieces three inches long. If the eel is very thick make two insertions on each side of the piece to facilitate cooking. Sprinkle with salt, roll in flour, brush with beaten egg, coat with browned breadcrumbs and fry in butter.

As the eel itself is fat not much butter is needed. To cook the eel through will take about 20 minutes.

JELLIED EEL

This is a very popular dish in Scandinavia. Wash, skin and dry the eel, which should weigh rather more than 1 lb., and divide into pieces three inches long. Make a mixture of 1 cup of vinegar to every 5 cups of water (sufficient to cover the eel), add a large chopped onion, 5 bayleaves, 10 peppercorns and 1 teaspoonful salt, and boil *without eel* for 5 minutes. Put in the eel and cook until tender (about 1 hour), skimming as necessary. Allow the eel to cool in the stock. Remove and place in a mould. Strain the stock through a cloth or jelly bag. Add gelatine in the proportion of 8 sheets or 1 oz. to every pint of stock, and when cool pour over the eels. If a clear jelly is desired, *before adding the gelatine* boil the stock with the white and crushed shell of an egg to every pint of the liquid for ten minutes and strain as before.

White wine used instead of water is a great improvement even for boiling eels, and always use English malt vinegar if this is available.

SCRAMBLED EGG

The Danes distinguish between *røræg*, which belongs to the scrambled egg family, and *æggestand* which is really an unsweetened baked egg custard. In particular the latter invariably accompanies smoked eel, often boiled ham. Perhaps it would take a Dane to explain why. Though doubtless less tidy-looking, *røræg* (scrambled egg) tastes much better (particularly, let it be said *sotto voce*, if no milk, cream or water is added to the beaten egg). Here, however, are Danish recipes for the two:

Røræg is made by adding a good dessertspoonful of cream or milk to each beaten egg, pouring the mixture into a saucepan in which a little butter has been melted and then stirring with a spoon until the scrambled egg has set but without becoming dry. This can only be achieved by scraping the mixture from the bottom and sides of the saucepan as it sets and by removing the pan from the fire before the last drops of liquid egg have set.

Æggestand is made by mixing with lightly beaten egg an equal quantity of milk or cream and pouring the mixture into a buttered tin (a rectangular cake tin, for example) and baking in a slow oven until set. When cold the egg is cut in strips as long as the bread upon which it is to be placed and about ½ inch wide and high.

DANISH GHERKINS

are robust fellows, much larger than the finger-sized gherkins which are often seen elsewhere. They should be well washed and, if they are as thick as they generally are, they should also be pricked in about half a dozen different places before being covered with salt overnight. Proceed as for Pickled Cucumbers (page 90).

DANISH HAMBURGERS (HAKKEBØFFER)

Shape minced raw beef into round, not too flat, cakes with a knife. Avoid packing too tight. Fry golden brown in butter or fat. The Danes prefer them well done but they are even better when pink inside. For *smørrebrød* cut in slices when cold and garnish with fried onions.

HERRING IN HEERING

Soak fillets of fat Icelandic spiced herring in milk for 8 hours before placing them in a marinade consisting of about ¾ Cherry

Heering and ¼ tomato purée to which French-type mustard, Worcester sauce and malt vinegar have been added.

The herring can now be served either as whole fillets or these can be cut in pieces. Immediately before serving garnish with a border of finely grated, fresh, peeled cucumber dipped in lemon juice or with tomato slices. Any other form of garnish such as parsley, dill, paprika etc. should be shunned as it would tend to impair the colour scheme.

MARINATED HERRINGS

Soak four salt herrings in milk. If they are very salt they may require 8 hours but never longer or they will be watery. Skin, bone, clean and place the fillets in a marinade of ¼ pint water, ¼ pint vinegar, preferably that which has been used for beetroot, 4 dessertspoonfuls of sugar, a little ground pepper, dill, chopped onion and 3 bayleaves. Allow to remain for at least 4 hours or, better, overnight.

SOUSED FRIED HERRING

Wash and remove the scales, fins and tails of as many fat herrings as are required. Remove the heads and degut. Press firmly on the back and sides of the fish with two fingers and, if the fish is truly fat, the bones should come out with ease when pulled by the other hand. Clean and wash the inside of the fish (which has not been slit open!) and dry with a cloth. Roll in flour and a little salt and fry in butter or margarine. When cool allow to remain overnight in the following marinade which is sufficient for 10 herrings:

½ pint vinegar, ¼ pint water, a little pepper, ½ teaspoonful of salt, 2 good dessertspoonfuls sugar, two large chopped onions. When serving garnish with raw onion rings and chopped parsley.

SPICED HERRINGS

These are the herrings used for making the famous Danish *gaffelbidder*. If Icelandic spiced herrings are available this part of the proceedings can be skipped. Ready-to-eat *gaffelbidder* are available in many countries in cans (see page 108). If you start with raw herrings this is the procedure: Wash and remove heads from the herrings. Soak overnight in a mixture of vinegar and water sufficient to cover the herrings. Make a salt and spice mixture of 2 lbs. salt, ½ lb. sugar, ½ lb. cornflour, a handful of Spanish hops, ½ oz. sandel, 2 handfuls of bayleaves, 1 oz. black peppercorns, 1 oz. allspice. This quantity should be sufficient for 80–100 herrings. Remove the herrings from the vinegar and place them, back downwards, on a layer of the salt-and-spice mixture. Proceed with alternate layers of mixture and herrings, the top layer being of the mixture. Apply pressure until the mixture turns into brine. Allow to stand for at least three weeks. Before using the herring should be boned and cleaned but not washed.

GOOSE LIVERPASTE

What goes into a tin labelled Pâté de Foie Gras or merely Pâté de Foie is a trade secret. The animal part of it is certainly not 100 per cent. gooseliver in any country. An excellent goose liverpaste can be made by mincing finely together a single gooseliver with an equal weight of fat pork, a small bayleaf, an apple, a small shallot and five anchovies. Pass through a hair sieve and add salt, pepper, a little ginger, beaten egg and a little cream. Bake slowly in a fireproof dish for about 1 hour. An offering of finely chopped truffle added before baking will make the result even more luxurious.

MISS KNUDSEN'S LIVERPASTE

Put 2 lbs. of pigs' liver and a little pickled herring three times through the grinder. Put 1½ lbs. of fat pork (no lean) twice through the grinder. Melt 2 dessertspoonfuls of butter and mix in an equal quantity of flour. To this add the ground pork fat and cook well. Add 5 beaten eggs and lastly the liver, pepper and salt. Place the paste in a form (an oblong cake tin, for example), stand the tin in a pan of water and bake for one hour in the oven.

MAYONNAISE

For the benefit of those who never knew or have forgotten how to make mayonnaise here is the basic recipe with some advice as to what you should do when things go wrong. The oil should be best olive oil and the eggs should be not less than one nor more than three or four days old. Break two eggs, separating every bit of the white from the yolk. In winter a single egg yolk will give mayonnaise for 2–3 persons, in summer it is better to use two yolks. It is best that all the ingredients, including the bowl, should not be cold or at least be at the same temperature. Put the egg yolk(s) in a bowl and add the oil a drop at a time, stirring continuously with a wooden spoon or beating with a whisk or beater. Should the oil and the egg refuse to bind the accepted thing to do is to take another egg yolk in another basin and start all over again, using your first effort drop by drop instead of pure oil. If the mayonnaise gets too thick it can be thinned with a little vinegar (tarragon maybe). After this it will take more oil if necessary. Season with salt and pepper.

There are many kinds of mayonnaise useful to know in connection with *smørrebrød:*

1) *Curry Mayonnaise* is made by simply adding a little curry powder to the prepared mayonnaise.

2) *Red Mayonnaise* looks and tastes good with lobster. Mix in the coral (roe) of a female lobster and add a little juice from grated, pressed beetroot. Another kind of red mayonnaise can be made by merely adding tomato ketchup.

3) *Horseradish Mayonnaise,* sometimes served with cold boiled fish or boiled beef, is made by adding, immediately before serving, a good spoonful or more of very finely grated horseradish to a cup of mayonnaise.

4) *Remoulade* too is based on mayonnaise (see also page 100).

5) *Béarnaise* can, if wanted cold at least, be based on mayonnaise (see page 89).

MEATBALLS (FRIKADELLER)

In a million and a half Danish households nearly every housewife will make *frikadeller* once a week. Some will use pigmeat, others veal, some half and half. Others again use beef and veal or maybe beef, veal and pigmeat. Housewife 1 will put the meat through the mincer or grinder once and mix it with water and white of egg, housewife 2 will put the meat through the machine twice or three times and use milk and egg yolk. Some will mix in breadcrumbs, other crushed rusk. Some will include grated onion, others not . . . and so almost *ad infinitum.* The ingredients, the methods and the results vary from home to home. Below are two recipes:

1) *Oskar Davidsen's frikadeller*
Put 1 lb. of pork and 1 lb. of veal twice through the grinder. Mix in 4 oz. of flour, finely chopped onion, 3 whole eggs,

⁷/₈ of a pint of milk, salt and pepper to taste. Stir exceeding well. If you want the *frikadeller* to be light in consistency the egg whites should be whisked and a little finely crushed rusk be added instead of some of the flour.

2) *Kaj's frikadeller*
require half pigmeat and half veal. The pigmeat should contain some fat and, as it must be able to hold together, the veal should be shank or some part of the animal with similar qualities. The meat must be put through the mincer (grinder) 3–4 times. To 1 ½ lbs. of meat stir in one whole beaten egg and a piled dessertspoonful of flour to help bind the mixture. A little, but not much, more flour may be added. The mixture is now stirred and stirred and stirred with milk. This stirring, easy for those with electric mixers, is the great secret of *frikadeller*. It is best that the mixture be allowed to rest for half an hour between stirrings. Immediately before the *frikadeller* are to be fried, in butter or margarine, stir well again, add salt, pepper, plenty of grated onion and then sodawater (the gassy stuff which most Sassenachs mix with their whisky). This makes the *frikadeller* light. Now is the time to fry a trial meatball. If too little flour has been used the meat will stick to the pan. In this case add a little more flour. They should be light and airy (this depends on the duration of the stirring), smooth in texture (this depends on the number of times the meat has been through the grinder), crisp on the outside and juicy inside (for this plenty of liquid is necessary).

MEAT JELLY

This recipe is used by Miss Knudsen who has been with Oskar Davidsen's for over a quarter of a century and is now *chef de cuisine*. It can be modified by the housewife at will.

OPPOSITE: *Junior's lunch: Cheese, raisins, apple, hardboile*
egg with chives. All are on rye bread

Split a knuckle of beef. Add scraps of sinewy or otherwise discarded beef. Brown well in the oven or in an iron stewpan. Cover with water. Add a bouquet-garni (thyme, parsley and bayleaf) plus onions, carrots, celery or celeriac, leeks and simmer for 4–5 hours in a covered stewpan. Add salt and peppercorns. After simmering for a further half hour add, if liked, a little garlic. Pass through a sieve and add 12–15 sheets of gelatine per quart of liquid (more will be required in summer than in winter). Add gravy browning as required. Clarify by adding one *lightly* beaten white of egg per quart of liquid. Strain through a cloth. If liked, at little port, sherry or madeira may now be added. Port is excellent if the meat jelly is to accompany goose liverpaste.

Allow the jelly to set and cut in strips or chop as required.

An excellent quick meat jelly can be made by boiling for 10 minutes in 1 cup (3 gills) of water: 1 small, sliced onion, 1 bayleaf, parsley, a meat cube, a dab of beef extract, a little coarsely ground pepper, a dash of celery salt. Add colouring and finally dissolve 3 leaves of gelatine in the mixture. Strain through a cloth and leave to cool in a square dish (a pie dish will do, a photographic developing dish is ideal). Place in the refrigerator until wanted.

PORK, SMOKED SADDLE OF (HAMBURGERRYG)

The part of the Danish bacon pig which in Britain becomes prime back rashers, in Denmark becomes the very characteristic and delicious *hamburgerryg*, first slightly salted, then lightly smoked. It can then be eaten in thin slices without any further cooking, or boiled and eaten hot or cold. For most people it will be more convenient to buy this Danish speciality in tins (see page 109). For those who keep hogs or wish to experiment themselves, here is the recipe:

Remove the greater part or all of the fat from a saddle of pork and detach the meat from the bones. Make a brine using 1 lb. of salt to each 3 pints of boiling water, add 1 bayleaf, 2 peppercorns and a good pinch of saltpeter per lb. of salt. When the brine is cold put the pork in it for 24 hours. It should then be cold-smoked for 12 hours. After this it is ready for boiling for about 45 minutes. At the end of this time let the pork remain in the liquid until cold or it may become dry.

REMOULADE

In Denmark remoulade is one of the most popular sauces but it differs from the sauce usually known by this name elsewhere. In its simplest Danish form remoulade consists of nothing more or less than finely chopped piccalilli to which mayonnaise and finely chopped parsley have been added. Another method is to stir French mustard, finely chopped shallots, finely chopped parsley and a few drops of lemon juice into some mayonnaise. A third way is to add French mustard, chopped capers, finely chopped gherkin and tarragon or parsley to a stiff mayonnaise. Another school of thought demands that there should be hard-boiled egg yolk in the mayonnaise in addition to the other ingredients.

SALMON MAYONNAISE

Remove the skin and bone from some cold fresh salmon, flake the fish and place in mayonnaise, thinned if necessary with the stock in which the salmon has been boiled or a little tarragon vinegar. Just before serving add fresh diced cucumber. Garnish with strips of anchovy, if liked, and strips of gherkin.

CHICKEN SALAD

Remove the skin from a roast or boiled chicken and chop the meat coarsely. Add to mayonnaise with a few canned mushrooms and a little shredded apple. Garnish with chopped egg and pieces of chicken breast. The salad must not be too stiff and if necessary should be thinned with a little of the liquid from the mushrooms.

CUCUMBER SALAD

No salad could be easier to prepare than this. The thinly-sliced cucumber (peeled or unpeeled according to personal choice) is placed in a bowl and covered with a mixture of lukewarm water and vinegar (at Davidsen's they prefer malt vinegar to the white wine vinegar more common on the Continent). The mixture should be sweetened to taste with sugar, and lemon juice may be used instead of vinegar. Add pepper and salt to taste and do not let the salad stand for more than half an hour before serving or the crispness of the cucumber will be lost. The liquid remaining can be used again by the addition of more cucumber.

CURRY SALAD

The basis of curry salad is half-inch pieces of cold, boiled macaroni mixed with a stiff mayonnaise into which curry powder has been stirred to taste. The mayonnaise can be seasoned with pepper and salt only or with a little lemon juice, a suspicion of grated onion and a little tomato ketchup. To the mixture can be added either small pieces of spiced or ordinary pickled herring (recipes for these on page 95) or thin strips of tongue and strips of celery or celeriac no thicker than a match-

stick. Curry salad is usually served in a bowl lined with crisp
lettuce leaves and is decorated with cress (if there are no cress-
haters around) and a slice or two of hardboiled egg.

HERRING SALAD

Take 1–2 pickled herrings, 3–4 floury boiled potatoes and a
pickled beetroot, put through a mincer or grinder and mix in a
little French-type mustard. Be sure there is sufficient beetroot to
make the salad a handsome red! If too stiff add a little beetroot
vinegar.

NORWEGIAN HERRING SALAD

Soak a few fillets of salt herring in water for about half an hour.
Chop a raw onion and some pickled cucumber (*asie*) and place
in a marinade of the cucumber vinegar, sugar and pepper. Add
the herring fillets and allow to stand for three hours.

ITALIAN SALAD

This Danish concoction has nothing to do with Italy and may
be compared with what is known as Russian salad in other
countries. Into a good, stiff mayonnaise put small pieces of
cold, boiled macaroni plus small cubes of boiled carrot and
peas. Asparagus too can be used.

LOBSTER SALAD

To some thick mayonnaise add a little tarragon vinegar and
mix with small pieces of cold, freshly cooked or canned lobster
and add pieces of asparagus, shredded lettuce, sliced egg and
tomato. Crab can be used instead of lobster. So can the small,
pink-shelled Norway lobsters.

SHRIMP SALAD

Though it is certainly not the case with a straightforward shrimp sandwich, canned shrimps are, according to the experts, better for shrimp salad than fresh shrimps. This is because the liquid in which they are preserved can be used to flavour the mayonnaise. Take a good thick mayonnaise and flavour it with a little shrimp liquid. Add the shrimps and some canned, fresh or cooked asparagus tips.

VEGETABLE SALAD

The way in which this salad can be prepared are legion. The Oskar Davidsen recipe is on page 40. Here is another: Whisk together a dessertspoonful of salad oil, a dessertspoonful of sugar, ½ teaspoon each of salt and mustard. Add three egg yolks one at a time, whisking all the while, and then 1 gill of thick, sour cream and ½ gill of vinegar. Cook slowly in a double saucepan until the mixture thickens. Allow to cool. To this mixture can be added raw white cabbage and walnuts or any other combination desired.

SALT VEAL OR BEEF

Known to the Danes simply as *salt kød* (salt meat), this is a delicious form of *pålæg*. Take a piece of fillet of veal or brisket or spare rib of beef and place in a dish. Rub into the meat a mixture of 1 oz. of coarse sugar, 3 oz. salt, ½ oz. saltpetre. Turn the meat and rub it with the mixture every day for a week. Remove the meat and if it appears too salt place it in cold water, otherwise in lukewarm. Bring to the boil slowly, skimming as necessary, and cook gently. Fillet of veal will require about 20 minutes and brisket about one hour depending on the weight of the meat. The spare rib should be cooked until the bones are loose enough to be removed. If the meat is allowed to remain in the water in which it has been cooked until cold it will not become dry. Alternatively the brisket or ribs can be removed and pressed between two boards.

ROLLED PRESSED SAUSAGE

Though usually made of pork, *rullepølse* can also be made of beef, veal or lamb. Remove the skin from a piece of pork belly, beat it out well and sprinkle with ½ teaspoonful of allspice and powdered cloves, 2 teaspoonfuls of pepper, 4 teaspoonfuls of salt and 2 grated onions. For those who prefer a less spicy sausage, salt and a little allspice only can be used. Roll up firmly, sew together and bind with twine. Rub into the meat a mixture of 1 oz. coarse sugar, 3 oz. salt, ½ oz. saltpetre. Turn the meat and rub the mixture into it every day for a week. Wash the meat and boil for about an hour. Put under pressure while cooling.

SWEETBREADS, CALF'S OR LAMB'S

First blanch the sweetbreads to make them firm and white. This is done by soaking them for at least an hour in cold water to remove the blood. Then place in a saucepan, cover with cold water and bring slowly to the boil. Simmer for a few minutes. Transfer to a basin of cold water and allow to remain until cold. Once the blanching process is over place the sweetbreads in a stewpan and add a little onion, carrot and turnip, season to taste and simmer gently for about 40 mins. for calf's or 20 mins. for lamb's sweetbreads. Press between two plates until cold. The sweetbreads can now be cut in slices for use as *pålæg* or they can be sliced, brushed with egg, rolled in seasoned flour or dried breadcrumbs and fried in fat until browned.

Some Danish Drinks

If quantity consumed is to be the yardstick, beer has no rival as Denmark's national drink. By any other measure *akvavit*, also called *snaps*, has excellent claims to be similarly regarded. The Danes' consumption of beer, about 126 pints yearly per person, is on latest available statistics considerably greater than that of the United States and about seven-eighths that of the United Kingdom. Their consumption of spirits is on the other hand much the same as that of the U.K. but scarcely more than a quarter that of the U.S.

Danish beer, both in Denmark and abroad, is almost synonymous with the products of *Carlsberg* and *Tuborg* (Denmark's two largest breweries) whose beer is known all over the world and which between them are responsible for 95 % of Denmark's beer exports. But *Wiibroe*, of Elsinore, also exports excellent beer. From Copenhagen *Stjernen*, the Star Brewery, exports its Viking beer.

All these breweries produce special beer for export, slightly stronger than the standard beer which most of them sell on the home market. This variety of light-coloured beer is called "pilsner" in Denmark. If you ask for "lager" in Denmark you will get a dark beer. Unlike many varieties of English beer, Danish pilsner should be drunk cold. It should be stored at 50 degrees Fahrenheit and drunk at 50–55 degrees.

Of *akvavit* or *snaps* there are several varieties on sale in Denmark. All are distilled by the Danish Distilleries which have the sole right of producing spirits in Denmark. "Aalborg Akvavit" is the *snaps* type normally served in restaurants and found at grocers etc. Other varieties have to be asked for by name and are not always in stock. "Aalborg Akvavit" (Aalborg is the town where this elixir is distilled) is the only Danish *snaps* which is exported. Other varieties on sale in Denmark include "Jubilæums Akvavit" and "Extra Akvavit". Both, the former in particular, are a little sweeter and smoother to the palate than ordinary "Aalborg Akvavit".

The most important thing about drinking *snaps* is that it *must* be drunk *very* cold. Only then is it a real pleasure to drink. Although it has, outside Denmark, been successfully used as a basis for cocktails *snaps* is, in its homeland, always drunk as an accompaniment to food, particularly with *smørrebrød*, and especially with herring and cheese. Only on rare occasions, and with a very limited range of dishes, is it drunk with hot food.

Snaps is served in extremely small glasses. It is a good idea to chill the glasses before use. Snaps should not be sipped but tossed back, half or a whole glass at a time. Beer is invariably served at the same time as snaps, the former often being used as a chaser for the latter. It is however considered more manly to content oneself with an "ah..hhh" and to take your punishment without quenching the fire in your throat with beer . . . Rather naturally greater quantities of Danish beer and snaps are consumed in Denmark than abroad. In the case of the Danes' third great alcoholic export, *Cherry Heering*, the contrary is the case. It will therefore be more appropriate for foreigners to instruct the Danes as to suitable occasions for the drinking of this world-famous Danish liqueur made since 1818 by the firm of Peter F. Heering. The Danes themselves find that it goes particularly well with cheese and not long ago Davidsen's produced a new delicacy—Herring in Heering (see recipe on page 93).

These then are the main Danish drinks to be found beyond the frontiers of Denmark. While it is true that the Danish Distilleries manufacture an excellent gin, neither this nor their whisky, also marketed in Denmark under the name of C.L.O.C., are at present available abroad.

Buying Danish Specialities

Since the first edition of this book appeared the western world has become truly *smørrebrød*-conscious. Whereas it had long been easy to find Danish butter, Danish bacon, Danablu cheese and Danish salami at your local grocer whether you lived in Slough, Singapore or Cincinnati, it was not until more recently that it became easy to find such Danish specialities as *gaffelbidder* (pickled herrings), *sylte* (brawn), smoked eel, *asier* (pickled cucumber), *hamburgerryg* (smoked pork), *frikadeller* (meatballs) etc. But within a few years there have been great changes. More than ever the world has become aware of the delights of Danish food and drink. To say nothing of Danish cutlery, furniture and many other fascinating products. Today we are pursued by spurious *smørrebrød* in many countries and the lowliest coffee bar or drugstore is inclined to offer "Danish pastries" which are the palest imitations of the real thing. The result of such development is that today you probably do not have to go further than your nearest supermarket for more or less any Danish speciality. In fact you may already be enjoying some of them without knowing that they are Danish. Many a foreigner must confess to enjoying his first Carlsberg or Tuborg without knowing that they were brewed in Denmark. Nowadays they probably are not anyway for their popularity has led to their being brewed elsewhere under licence.

If you do experience difficulty in obtaining any of the Danish products mentioned in this book you can be reasonably certain that a phone call or card to the nearest Danish consulate will produce the information you want. If not, you can be certain of getting some helpful advice if you write to The Danish Agricultural Marketing Board, Vester Farimagsgade 6, Copenhagen V., Denmark.

Index

(NB. The numbers indicated are page numbers).

Colour photographs by Niels Elswing. Linen, plate and tableware in the photographs of Oskar Davidsen's smørrebrød kindly lent by Den Permanente; kitchen utensils etc., in the remaining three photographs kindly lent by Illums Bolighus.